MW00787688

DOGS IN ENGLISH PORCELAIN

of the 19th Century

Dogs in English Porcelain

of the 19th Century

Dennis G. Rice

ANTIQUE COLLECTORS' CLUB

ISBN 1 85149 390 5

British Library Cataloguing-in-Publication Data
A catalogue record for this book is available from the British Library

Frontispiece: *Pair of Staffordshire black-spotted Dalmatians. See Colour Plate 196.*

Printed in the Czech Republic
Published in England by the Antique Collectors' Club Limited, Woodbridge, Suffolk IP12 4SD

Contents

Acknowledgements

I am much indebted to Christie's, Phillips and Sotheby's for their generous provision of photographs of porcelain dogs which have, over the years, passed through their salerooms and for permission to reproduce them and quote from their sale catalogues.

I am also indebted to those dealers and collectors who have kindly made photographs available to me and whose names appear in the captions beneath the relevant illustrations.

I must also express my appreciation to Mrs. Delia Napier, Mr. Robin Blackwood and Mr Gordon Clark for having brought to my attention the various discoveries they have made in the course of their extensive collecting.

I am also grateful to the Museum of Worcester Porcelain for allowing me to reproduce photographs of two dogs in their collection, to the Zoological Society of London for sending me a list of the breeds of domestic dogs kept at the London Zoo between 1827 and 1927, to Mrs. Audrey Dudson for her assistance in identification or possible identification of certain animals as being of Dudson origin, and to Mr. Anton Gabszewicz for informing me from time to time of various forthcoming auction sales of items relevant to this book.

My acknowledgements would not, however, be complete without recording the help and general encouragement in writing this book that I have received from my wife, to whom the subject matter has always presented a particular appeal.

Introduction

In this country in the nineteenth century, particularly in the first half, the breeds of dogs were less numerous than they are today. Moreover, in some instances, they assumed a somewhat different appearance, and consequently identification with their modern successors is not always easy. Nor is the difficulty necessarily resolved by resorting to contemporary engravings, as the following passage from Stables' *Our Friend the Dog*, published in 1895, shows:

> It is a common thing for writers on dogs to refer to old pictures, or engravings, in order to obtain information regarding the style of any breed of dog that obtained in by-gone times. But such information is often very misleading, for the simple reason that the artist, although a good painter, may have known nothing at all about the points of dogs. Few even of the brethren of the brush of now-a-days could tell a setter from a Sheepdog.
>
> For instance, the dog that stood for a Setter at page ninety in Youatt's book is a disgrace to the text; he resembles a Landseer Newfoundland, with bad legs, and

stern; he is stilty in fore-legs and wears a Collie's head with a Spaniel's ears.

Dogs of the nineteenth century in this country can conveniently be divided into (i) useful dogs and (ii) pets.

The former can be sub-divided into sporting and non-sporting dogs. Sporting dogs were valued for their services in the field, and although doubtless some were also companionable, they lived, when at home, out of doors in the kennel. They included the greyhound, the spaniel (springer, cocker and water), the setter, the pointer, the poodle (or rough water dog) and, of course, the foxhound. The useful non-sporting dogs included, among others, the great Dane (or Danish dog) and the Dalmatian, both of which were employed to accompany and watch over carriages, the Newfoundland and the mastiff, both guard dogs, the former with a remarkable ability to rescue people from drowning and, of course, the all important sheepdog (or, as it was originally called, the 'shepherd's dog').

Pet dogs included the Italian greyhound, the King Charles spaniel (sometimes called 'the comforter'), the pug and the poodle. It will be seen that the poodle appears in both classifications – as a sporting dog and as a pet.

All the above breeds came to be represented in English porcelain of the nineteenth century.[1]

Other breeds, co-existing with the aforementioned, e.g. the lurcher, the cur, the turnspit and the Maltese dog, do not seem to appear in porcelain, and accordingly no mention will be found of them in the following pages. One breed, however, which seems never to have been produced in porcelain is worthy of remark – the bulldog (an animal, incidentally, quite different in shape from its modern-day counterpart). It was, in the period with which we are concerned, unlike today's bulldog, noted for its ferocity and tenacity. It received a bad press, as the following contemporary comments illustrate:

> The round, thick head, turned-up nose, and thick and pendulous lips of this dog are familiar to all, while his ferocity makes him in the highest degree dangerous. In general he makes a silent although ferocious attack and the persistent powers of his teeth and jaws enable him to keep his hold against any but the greatest efforts, so that the utmost mischief is likely to ensure as well to the innocent visitor of his domicile as the ferocious intruder. The bull-dog is scarcely capable of any education and is fitted for nothing but ferocity and combat.[2]

Not surprisingly, the breed, with its association with bull-fighting, did not commend itself to those most likely to purchase porcelain animals, namely children and ladies. No factory will produce what it cannot sell easily.

As this book will show, there were other breeds of dog intrinsically more acceptable to the market, and the various porcelain manufacturers preferred to direct their attention to this more attractive field.

The dating of the dogs illustrated here inevitably presents considerable difficulty. Normally, any degree of precision is impossible and one is constrained to resort to a wide period. For example, in the case of Staffordshire dogs, all that can be said is that normally they were not produced before 1835 (occasionally 1830) and not significantly later than 1850. In some instances it is unlikely the animal was produced before 1840, and the time bracket has been shortened accordingly. However, it cannot be over-emphasised that all dates given are no more than approximations.

Dog Models
and their
Factories of Origin

This section illustrates the breeds of dog represented in English porcelain in the nineteenth century. Individual manufacturers are grouped under each breed.

GREYHOUNDS

Greyhounds have been in this country for centuries and can be traced back to the time of the Roman occupation. In 1496 the qualities looked for in a greyhound were expressed in verse by Wynkyn de Worde:

> A greyhound should be headed lyke a snake,
> And neckyd lyke a drake,
> Fotyd lyke a cat,
> Tayled lyke a ratte,
> Syded like a teme
> And chyned like a bream.[1]

During the eighteenth century the greyhound was remodelled. Although in its existing form it enjoyed good looks, it lacked speed and stamina, qualities essential for the purpose for which it was required, namely hare-coursing. The strain of other breeds was introduced including, in particular, that of the bulldog noted for its ferocity and tenacity.

Greyhounds were much prized by sportsmen and the first tomb erected for a dog in this country commemorated an eighteenth century 'Snowball', one of a litter of three outstanding examples of the breed. Major Topham of the World Cottage, Yorkshire, wrote an epitaph for 'Snowball' which included these lines:

> He who out-bounded time and space
> The fleetest of the greyhound race
> Lives here! At length subdued by death
> His speed now stopped and out of breath.

Greyhounds normally hunted the hare in pairs. The technique employed is described by Youatt in *The Dog*:[2]

> In the *Sportsman* for April 1840 there is an interesting account of the chace of the hare. It is said that, in general, a good greyhound will reach a hare, if she runs straight. He pursues her eagerly, and the moment he is about to strike at her she turns short, and the dog, unable to stop himself, is thrown from ten to twenty yards from her. These jerking turns soon begin to tell upon a dog, and an old well-practised hare will seldom fail to make her escape. When, however, pursued by a couple of dogs, the hare has a more difficult game to play, as it frequently happens that when she is turned by the leading dog she has great difficulty in avoiding the stroke of the second.

> It is highly interesting to witness the game of an old hare. She has generally some brake or thicket in view, under the cover of which she means to escape from her pursuers. On moving from her seat she makes directly for the hiding-place, but, unable to reach it, has recourse to turning, and *wrenched* by one or other of her pursuers, she seems every moment almost in the jaws of one of them, and yet in a most dexterous manner she accomplishes her object. A greyhound, when he perceives a hare about to enter a thicket, is sure to strike at her if within any reasonable distance. The hare shortens her stride as she approaches the thicket, and at the critical moment she makes so sudden, dexterous and effectual a spring, that the dogs are flung to a considerable distance, and she has reached the cover and escaped.

Mention must also be made of the Italian greyhound, a miniature of the greyhound just described, but with a somewhat more arched neck and with a high stepping action, rather like that of a well-trained carriage horse. As the name suggests, the breed was imported into this country from Italy. Italian greyhounds are not suited to kennel life but require comfort and companionship. In other words, they are lap-dogs, not sporting dogs. Bewick speaks of the breed as being 'not common in this country, the climate being too rigorous for the extreme delicacy of its constitution'.[3] William Taplin[4] gave the breed an even more damning press:

> This diminutive breed . . . seems only calculated to soothe the vanity, and indulge the frivolities of antiquated ladies . . . They are so deficient in the spirit, fortitude and self-defence of every other sort of the canine race, as not to be able to officiate in the services of domestic alarm or protection, and in consequences are dedicated only to the comforts of the tea-table, the fire-side carpet, the luxurious indulgencies of the sofa and the warm lap of the mistress.[5]

Confirmation of the frailties of the Italian greyhound can be found in the vivid account of her pet given by Mrs. Sherwood (1775–1851) in her diary:[6]

> My little greyhound at the time filled too much of my thoughts, and caused me to throw too many kind affections, which would have been far better employed on a poor fellow-creature. This beautiful little animal suffered so terribly from the cold, and had so many contrivances to warm itself, that it was impossible not to pity it. When we walked out it crept into my muff, and there it lay with its head only looking out. It often crept into my pocket or on my lap under my work, or into my workbasket, and when in the kitchen it always sat on the back of Lion, our great Newfoundland house-dog. I loved my little Bonne [the animal's name] so much that I resolved, after I lost her, never to make a pet of any animal.

Modern writers have pointed out that the Italian greyhound is perfectly suited to this climate and have challenged the accuracy of much of Taplin's criticism, but, be that as it may, the breed was popular in this country as a lap-dog at the end of the eighteenth century, vying with the pug dog for the affection of the ladies. (A specimen is to be seen in the famous painting of the *Ladies of Llangollen* returning from riding.) Italian greyhounds were said to be only suitable for women, hence the restriction on the numbers bred. Nevertheless, they were still popular during the 1830s.[7]

The importance of the greyhound as a sporting dog and a lap-dog is reflected in the frequency with which this particular breed is represented in various media.

Greyhounds, which incidentally hunt by sight, not by scent, appear in early Renaissance paintings and drawings, normally, in connection with stag hunting, for example in *The Vision of St. Eustace* (c.1440) by Pisanello,[8] *The Hunt* by Paolo Uccello (1397–1475),[9] *The Vision of St. Hubert* (1501) by Albrecht Dürer,[10] and *Diana the Huntress* (c.1540) from the School of Fontainebleau.[11]

They continued to be depicted in art throughout the seventeenth and eighteenth centuries, for example in *Starting for the Hunt* by Aelbert Cuyp (1620–1691),[12] and *Black Greyhound* (with a poodle) (1723) by Jean-Baptiste Oudry. In the late eighteenth and early nineteenth centuries, greyhounds regularly featured in paintings, as in Benjamin Marshall's painting of *Colonel Thornton's Greyhound*, and Philip Reinagle's painting of *Major*, winner of the Thousand Guinea Challenge Cup for coursing on Epsom Downs engraved by J. Scott for *The Sportsman's Cabinet*. From around 1840 onwards greyhounds were painted simply as cherished pets of their owners, Prince Albert's Eos, portrayed in 1841 by George Morley and Edwin Landseer respectively, being a prime example. Greyhounds also appear in porcelain.

Rockingham

The most important factory associated with animal production during our period is the Rockingham factory at Swinton, Yorkshire. This particular concern was responsible for a variety of breeds of dog, but surprisingly, I have never actually seen a Rockingham greyhound, a breed so important that its omission would be quite remarkable. However, I have come across evidence of its existence in the form of an auction description which reads: 'A Rockingham Figure of a Greyhound lying with its head supported on its forepaws on a base moulded with leaves, gilt border, 4½in. *impressed mark*'.[13] There is no reference to an incised number. Although this may possibly be due to neglect on the part of the cataloguer, it is more likely the case that this particular example did not actually have a number. Accordingly, we can in the light of the 'impressed mark' reasonably assume that the factory turned out a greyhound, but we cannot identify it by a number.

Interestingly, the Rockingham factory also produced a silhouette or flat-back figure, consisting of two white greyhounds, on a white and gilt rectangular base (Figure 1). Although this was not, strictly speaking, part of the factory's animal series, it reinforces the importance of greyhounds as a breed to be represented in porcelain.

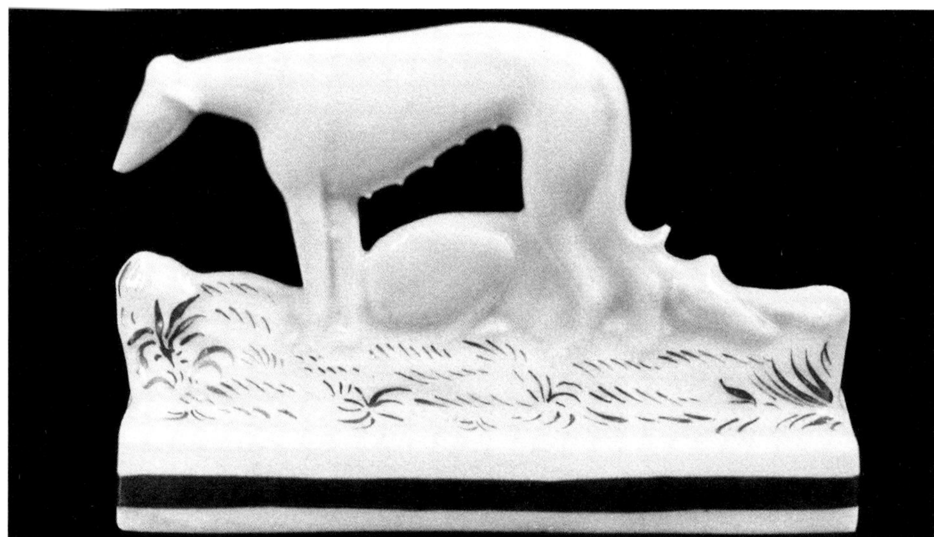

Figure 1. *Rockingham silhouette group of two white greyhounds on a white and gilt rectangular base. 2¹³⁄₁₆in. long. C. 1. Red Griffin mark. 1826–30.*

FIGURE 2. *Pair of Derby greyhounds, one with black and grey, the other with brown patches, each lying recumbent on a shaped base applied with flowers. 4¼in. long. Late eighteenth or early nineteenth century.* Christie's

Derby (Nottingham Road)

The standing greyhound model illustrated in Colour Plate 1 and Figure 3 is of Derby origin. Formerly, I thought it was a Minton product, albeit omitted from the factory drawing book. However, that it is in fact Derby, not Minton, has recently been established by the discovery of a Derby marked pointer standing on an almost identical base (Colour Plate 187). Manifestly, the pointer and the greyhound must have been made by the same factory, and as the pointer bore the Derby mark, it follows that the greyhound must also have had a Derby origin. Interestingly, there is an entry in Haslem's list of 'Bow and Chelsea Models'[14]:

	Enamelled and gilt
London Pointer and Greyhound, each	1s 6d

The thought suggests itself that the Derby pointer of Colour Plate 187 and the Derby greyhound of Colour Plate 1 and Figure 3 are the models there referred to. Their size is commensurate with the price ascribed to them in the list.

It is interesting to note that in the Print Room of the British Museum is an engraving of a greyhound (seemingly of 'Young Snowball') by C. Turner executed in 1810 after the painting by Jacques Laurent Agasse. The greyhound there depicted is the greyhound of Colour Plate 1 but in reverse.[15]

A fine pair of Derby greyhounds are illustrated in Figure 2. They are described by Christie's as: 'A FINE AND RARE PAIR OF DERBY FIGURES of recumbent greyhounds,

COLOUR PLATE 1. *Derby greyhound in grey standing with tree support on a deep oval base green with reddy-brown splashes, edged in white and gold. 2⅝in. high. c.1830. For another example see Figure 3.*

FIGURE 3. *Derby greyhound, the grey coat enriched with black patches, standing with tree stump support on a deep oval base in green edged in white and gold. 2¾in. high. c.1830. For another example see Colour Plate 1.*

Christie's South Kensington

their tails curled up round their hind legs, one with black and grey and the other with brown patch markings, the shaped rectangular mound bases applied with flowers – 4¼in. (11cm) wide'.[16] It is interesting to note that this same greyhound model appears lying at the feet of the Derby figure 'Diana, the Huntress', a figure originally produced in the eighteenth century[17] but carried on into the nineteenth century. Whether the greyhound as an independent model was also made in the nineteenth century is not known for certain. The pair appearing at Christie's could, from the description, have been from either the eighteenth or nineteenth century, but regardless of the date of that particular pair, it is reasonable to assume that, in accordance with its normal practice where eighteenth century animals were concerned, the factory continued producing these greyhounds into the nineteenth century. It is to be noted that Bemrose in his list of moulds and models existing in 1795 refers to 'Pair Greyhounds with ground pedestal'.

Derby (King Street)

This small factory is known to have turned out a pair of greyhounds recumbent on a rectangular base, one scratching, the other assuming a more dignified pose. Such a pair in biscuit are shown in Colour Plate 2. They bear the 'Crown S & H, crossed swords and D' mark in blue.

Chamberlain Worcester

The Chamberlain Worcester factory produced a recumbent greyhound model with crossed front legs, on a rectangular base with rounded corners, some 4in. long. An example with a matt-blue base, a colour typical of the factory, is illustrated in Figure 4.

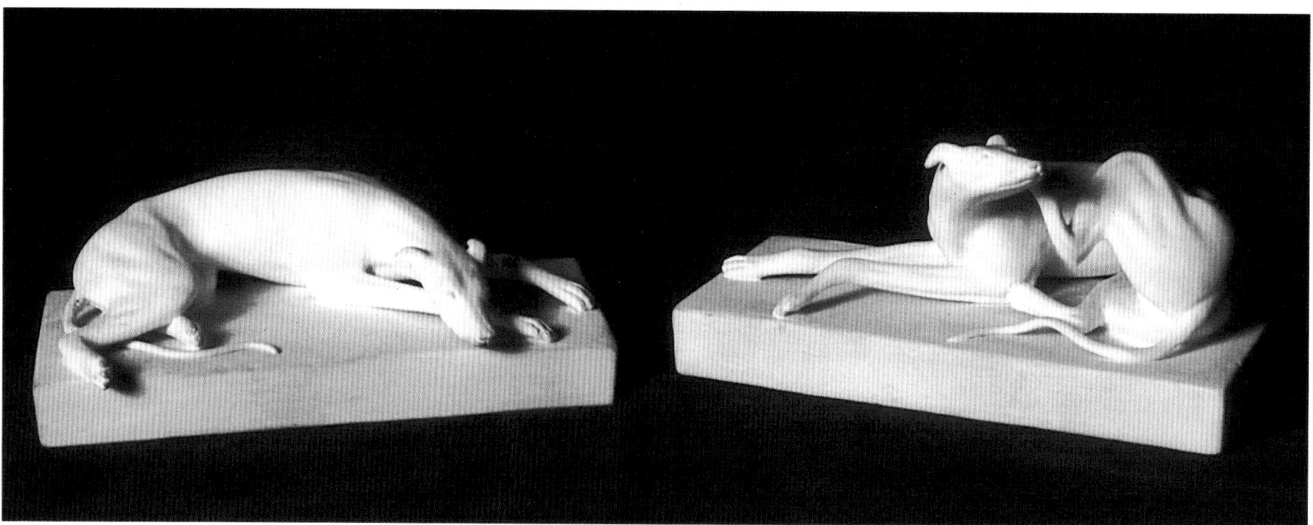

COLOUR PLATE 2. *Pair of biscuit greyhounds from the King Street factory, Derby. 5¼in. long. Sampson Hancock mark in blue. Later nineteenth century. For a Grainger Lee example see Colour Plate 8 (second row left)* Dr. J Freeman

FIGURE 4. *Chamberlain Worcester greyhound with crossed front legs, lying recumbent on a rectangular dry-blue base with rounded corners. 4in. long. Mark: 'Chamberlain Worcester' written in script c.1820–40.*
Godden of Worthing Ltd.

Doubtless, it was one of a pair. Another Chamberlain model is referred to by Sotheby's as 'A Chamberlain's Worcester Figure of a white greyhound sitting on a stepped canted rectangular base washed in pink, 3⅛in. "Chamberlains Worcester" in red script'.[18]

It should also be noted that greyhounds are mentioned in the factory documents:

4 Greyhounds and oak tree
2 Greyhounds at 4 – 0[19]

Grainger Lee & Co., Worcester

A pair of greyhounds appear in the factory's pattern book. Porcelain examples are illustrated in Colour Plates 3 and 8 (second row, left).

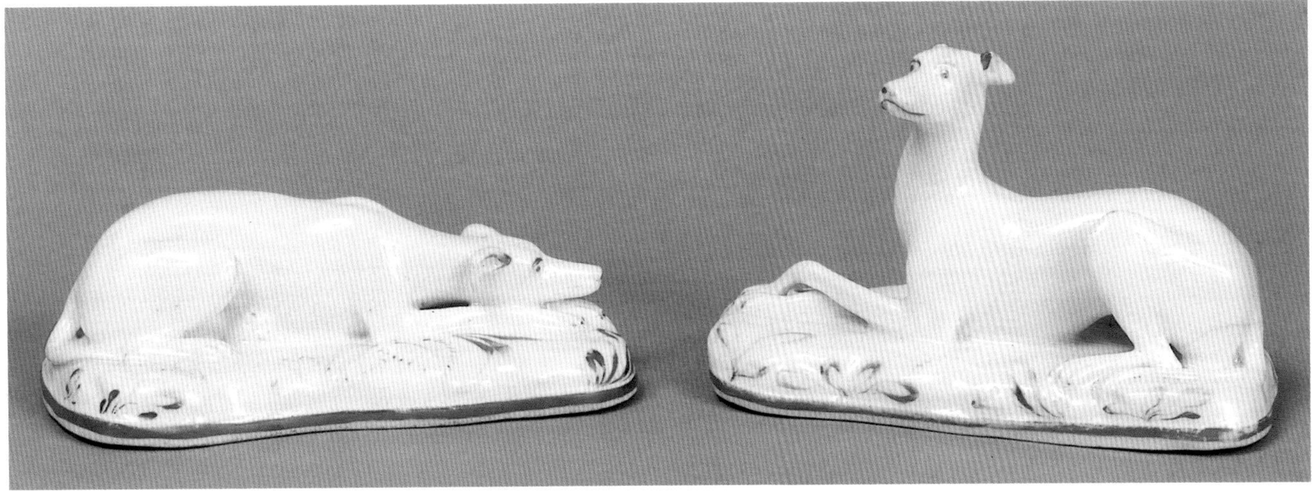

COLOUR PLATE 3. *Pair of Grainger Lee white and gilt greyhounds, lying recumbent on scrolled bases. 4½in. long. Impressed 'GRAINGER LEE & CO WORCESTER' in capitals. 1820–37. For another example see Colour Plate 8 (second row, left).*

Colour Plate 4. *Minton greyhound with black patches lying recumbent on a maroon and yellow cushion base with tassels. 4in. long. Model No 18. c.1831–40. For another example see Figure 5.* Andrew Dando Antiques

Royal Worcester

Early in its life, the Royal Worcester factory produced a group of greyhounds chained. It is item 33 in the factory's list.[20]

Minton

A white and gilt example of the Minton greyhound (No 18 in the factory drawing book) is shown in Figure 5. A coloured version appears in Colour Plate 4. The model was also produced in biscuit. Moreover, after about 1847 it was turned out in Parian. An example, together with a King Charles Spaniel (No 22 in the drawing book) is recorded in this body, additionally incised with the ermine mark.

Incidentally, it is interesting to record the favourable comment made in 1846 on Minton biscuit: 'The bisque figures of Messrs. Minton have enjoyed for a long time a very considerable sale . . . they are most carefully executed and were until lately the very best production of this class of art in the Potteries'.[21]

Colour Plate 5. *Minton fawn and white greyhound lying recumbent on a stippled crimson base with rounded corners. 3⅞in. long. Model No 18, but with a different base. c.1831–40.*

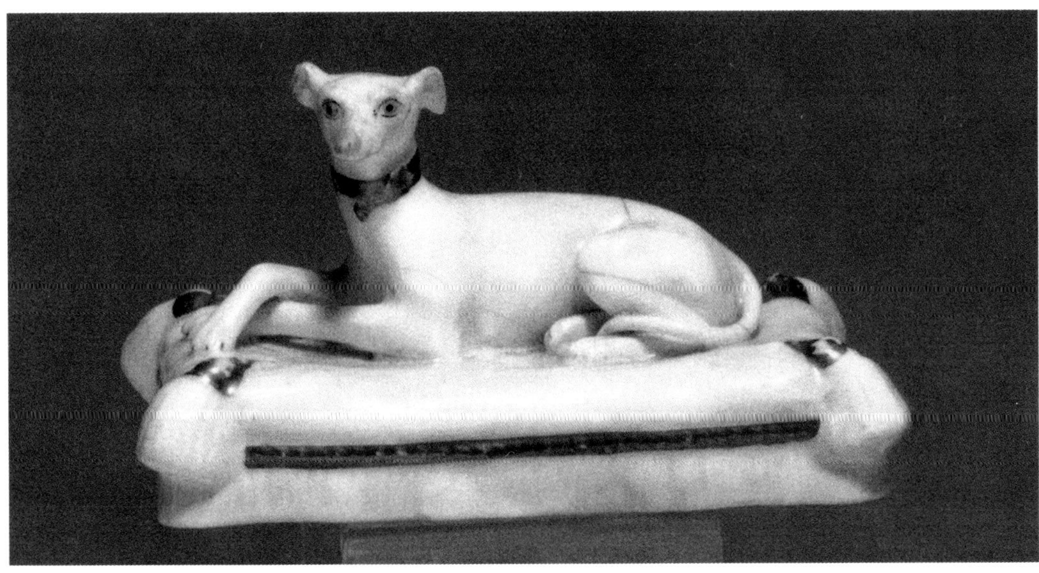

FIGURE 5. *Minton white and gilt greyhound lying recumbent on a cushion base with tassels. 4¼ in. long. Model No 18. c.1831–40. For another example see Colour Plate 4.*
Christie's South Kensington

Quite what was meant by the qualification 'until lately' is not clear. Biscuit did not begin to be replaced by Parian until the middle of 1847 and it was still being produced at the end of December 1847. But the favourable comments on Minton biscuit continued: 'Minton's bisque figures are now superior to the French in artistic management of drapery, and particularly in lace imitations, and he gives equal excellence at a cheaper rate'[22].

However, by 28 December 1847 there was a reluctance to continue with the biscuit formula. For in a letter of that date to George Sparks, the Worcester china decorater and retailer, the factory wrote: 'If the Ariadne would do in our Parian material instead of Bisque China, we could send it immediately . . . please let us know. The Parian is much preferred for statuary'. Although the greyhound model No 18 appears in the factory drawing book as lying on a cushion with tassels, it was also fashioned on a plain rectangular base with rounded corners.[23] An example is illustrated in Colour Plate 5. The same base variation is found in the case of the factory's pug dog – compare Colour Plate 34 with Colour Plate 35.

Presumably, the model shown in Colour Plates 4 and 33 (second row, right), and Figure 5 was not intended to represent an animal whose life was spent out of doors coursing hares. The element of comfort and luxury implicit in the tasselled cushion would seem to indicate that a lap-dog was meant, and accordingly this must have been an Italian greyhound. This conclusion is reinforced by the fact that other animals which the Minton factory modelled on a tasselled cushion, that is to say, a King Charles Spaniel (one version recumbent, another standing begging), a pug and two versions of a poodle, were in every case lap-dogs, and not sporting dogs. However, the position is not absolutely clear. For one version of the factory's setter, a purely sporting dog, is made to lie on a tasselled cushion rather than a plain rectangular base with scrolled decoration moulded around the edges (compare Colour Plate 171 with Colour Plate 172).

An interesting animal appearing in the Minton drawing book is

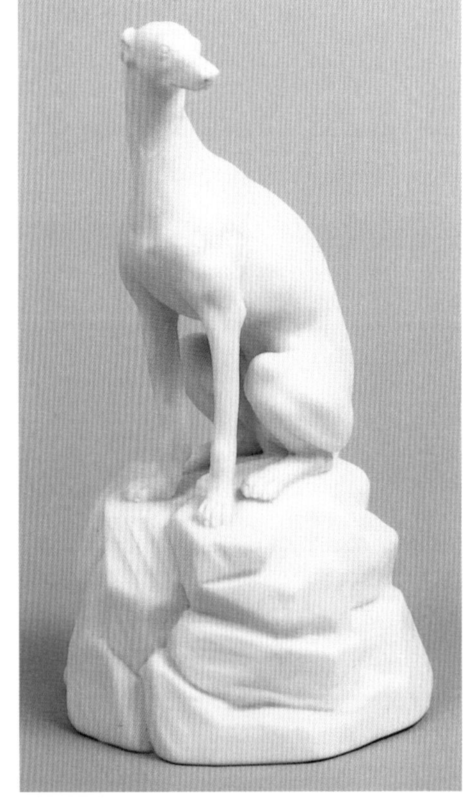

COLOUR PLATE 6. *Minton greyhound seated on a high rocky base, in Parian. 6½in. high. Model No 120. c.1850–70.*

COLOUR PLATE 7. *Pair of Copeland & Garrett greyhounds, one black one tan, each lying recumbent on a shallow mound base in green. 5in. long. Factory mark. 1833–47.*

No 120, a greyhound sitting upright on a high mound, 6½in. high in all. An example of that particular model is shown in Colour Plate 6. It is in fact in Parian, although the model was originally produced in biscuit porcelain. Notwithstanding that, in the original drawing book, model No 120 is entitled simply 'greyhound'; in the later Parian list of models, dated 1852, it is more specifically described as 'Italian Greyhound'. Clearly, once again the factory opted to produce a lap-dog rather than the larger sporting animal.

However, there is no reason to suppose that the large greyhound (No 130 in the factory list) in natural colours on a crimson and gilt base illustrated by Battie, is other than the ordinary English coursing greyhound. The model is indeed large, measuring 13¾in. high.[24]

FIGURE 6. *Copeland & Garrett greyhound bitch, recumbent on a rectangular base with shaped corners. 11in. long. Mark: 'Copeland & Garrett' within a wreath surmounted by a coronet. 1833–47.*

Godden of Worthing Ltd.

COLOUR PLATE 8. *First row. Copeland & Garrett tan-coloured greyhound scratching, lying recumbent on a green shaped rectangular base moulded with white and gilt scrolls. 5in. long. 1833–47. Compare the base with that of the factory's marked King Charles spaniel of Colour Plate 130.*
Second row (left). Grainger Lee greyhound lying recumbent with nose to the ground on a scrolled base. 4⅞in. long. 1820–37. Compare with the marked example of Colour Plate 3.
Second Row (right). Staffordshire greyhound with grey patches lying, with front paws crossed, on a shaped pink mound base. 5in. long. c.1835–50. Compare with the pair of dogs of Colour Plate 16. Christie's South Kensington

Copeland & Garrett

The Copeland & Garrett factory produced a large pair of greyhounds, each lying recumbent on a rectangular base with shaped corners. Illustrated in Figure 6 is the bitch. The reverse model, is, of course, the dog.

The factory also produced the pair of greyhounds shown in Colour Plate 7.

Although it is not marked, the scratching greyhound appearing in Colour Plate 8 (first row) is clearly of Copeland & Garrett origin. For the animal lies on a base identical in form to the marked base supporting the King Charles of Colour Plate 130.

COLOUR PLATE 9. *Pair of Samuel Alcock greyhounds with black patches, lying with crossed front paws on shaped pale-yellow rectangular bases moulded with scrolls. 3½ in. long. Impressed '201'. c.1840–50.*
Christie's South Kensington

Samuel Alcock

The greyhounds appearing in Colour Plate 9 impressed '201' are from the Samuel Alcock factory. So too is the greyhound impressed '93' appearing in Colour Plate 10. The group of Colour Plate 12 is in Parian, but a biscuit example can be seen in the Victoria and Albert Museum impressed '55' under the base. The group appears in the 1851 Exhibition Catalogue,[25] and it is clear from the relevant entry that it was modelled by S.W. Arnold. As the animals lie on a tasselled cushion, presumably they were intended to represent Italian greyhounds. They may have been based on unidentified marbles or bronzes.

These same dogs, albeit executed not as a group, but individually as a pair, are recorded in pottery[26] (Colour plate 13). As the Samuel Alcock factory produced earthenware as well as porcelain, perhaps the pottery dogs should also be attributed to the Samuel Alcock factory. The large biscuit greyhound of Colour Plate 11 commemorates a particular dog, 'Echo'.

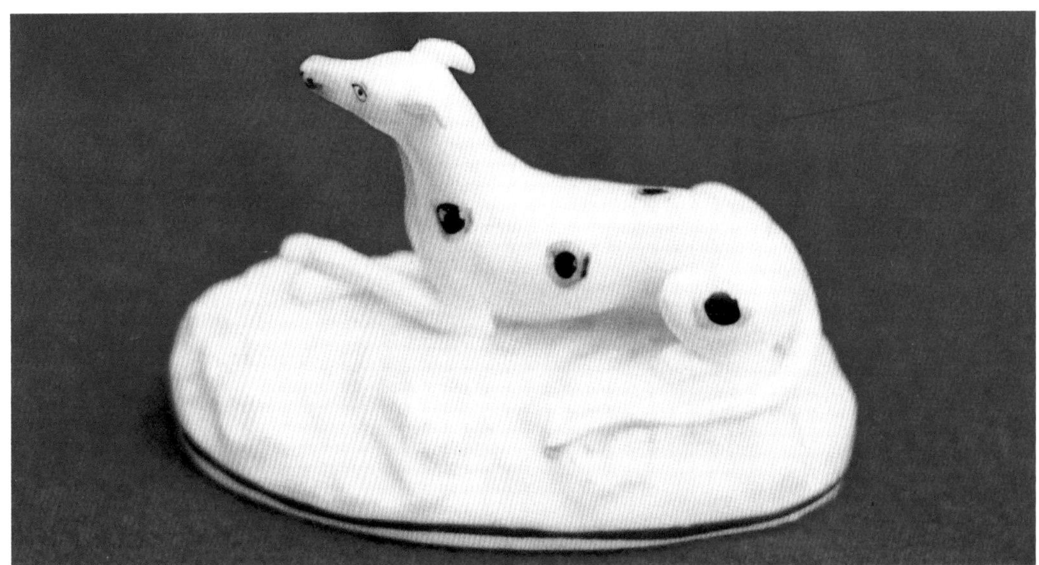

COLOUR PLATE 10. *Samuel Alcock greyhound lying recumbent on a yellow mound base. 4¼ in. long. Impressed '93'. c.1835–50.*
John Read Antiques

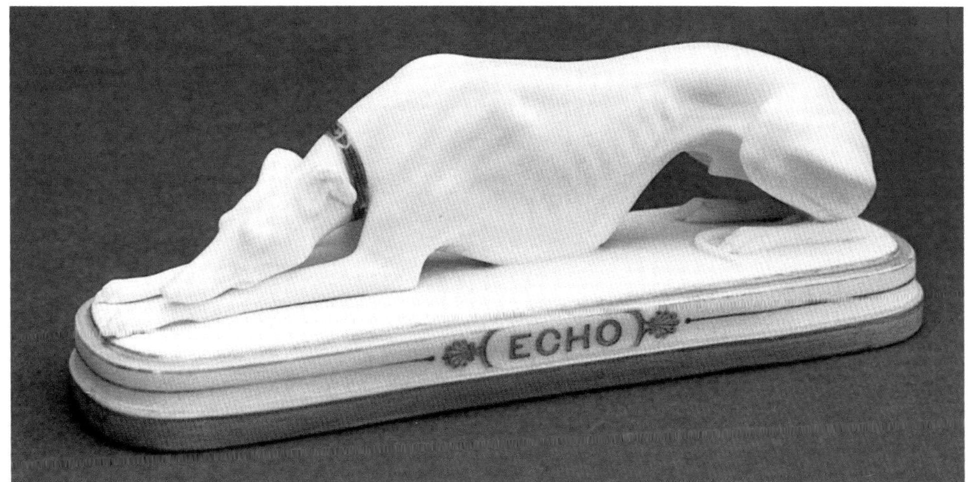

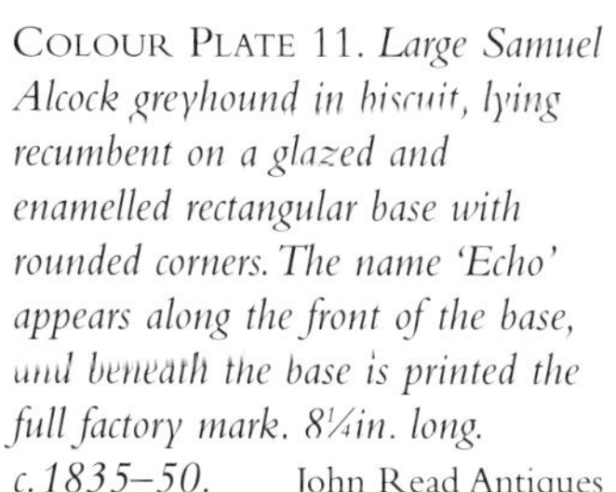

COLOUR PLATE 11. *Large Samuel Alcock greyhound in biscuit, lying recumbent on a glazed and enamelled rectangular base with rounded corners. The name 'Echo' appears along the front of the base, and beneath the base is printed the full factory mark. 8¼in. long. c.1835–50.* John Read Antiques

COLOUR PLATE 12. *Samuel Alcock model of a group of 'Chained Greyhounds' in Parian, consisting of a bitch elegantly poised, and a scratching dog, lying recumbent on a tasselled cushion and linked together with a chain (now missing). 7¼in. long. Model No 55 in the factory list. c.1850–70.*

COLOUR PLATE 13. *Pair of pottery greyhounds, also found in porcelain, with similar poses to those of the dogs of Colour Plate 12. 5in. long. Possibly from the Samuel Alcock factory. c.1835–50.*
John Read Antiques

COLOUR PLATE 14. *White and gilt greyhound seated on a dry-blue rectangular mound base with rounded corners. 3⅛in. high. Inscribed under the base in red '128'. Possibly Charles Bourne. Compare the greyhounds of Colour Plate 15. c.1825.*

Charles Bourne

A pair of seated greyhounds, from the Charles Bourne factory are illustrated in Colour Plate 15. They are each inscribed under the base with the number '10'. The dog of Colour Plate 14 is modelled in the same way as the pair, but is inscribed with the number '128' and has a differently constructed tail – all the tails incidentally would appear to be unrestored. It is difficult to believe that all three dogs do not come from the same factory.

COLOUR PLATE 15. *Pair of Charles Bourne greyhounds, each seated on a dry-blue rectangular base with rounded corners. 3¼in. high. Inscribed under the base '10' in red. 1817–30.*

COLOUR PLATE 16. *Pair of Staffordshire greyhounds, each lying recumbent on a green shallow mound base. 5in. long. c.1835–50. Compare the dog of Colour Plate 8 (second row, right).*

Unidentified Staffordshire Factories (Colour Plates 16–19)
Greyhounds were produced throughout Staffordshire during the period 1830–50, and examples are shown here. The cross-legged pair of Colour Plate 18, together with the single specimen also there illustrated, lie on the same shaped scrolled base used to support the poodles of Colour Plates 19b and 96 and the spaniel of Colour Plate 147, indicating a common factory of origin.

COLOUR PLATE 17. *Staffordshire greyhound bitch lying recumbent on a matt-blue shallow mound base. 5in. long. c.1835–50.*

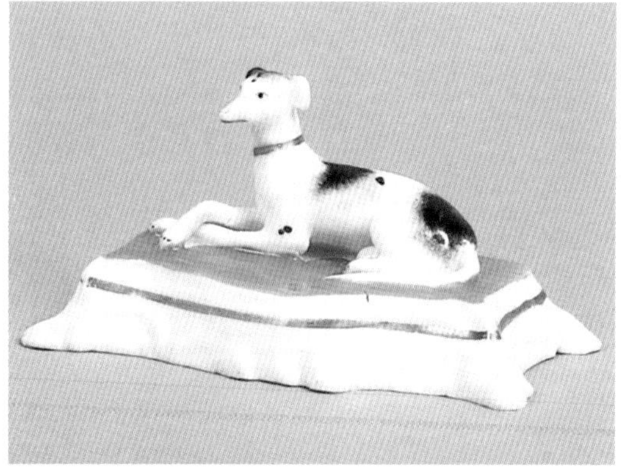

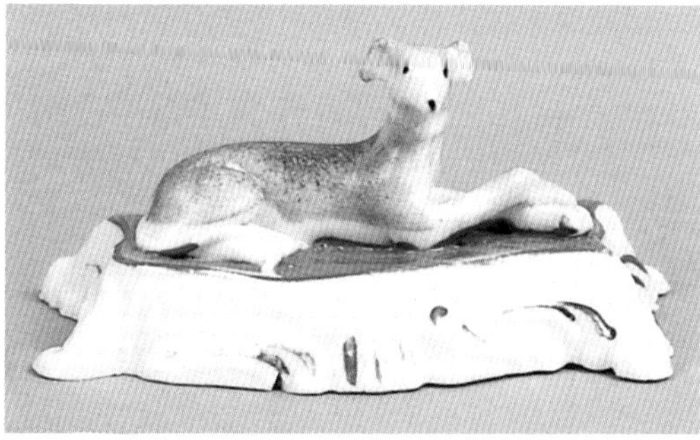

COLOUR PLATE 18. *Pair of Staffordshire greyhounds with brown patches, each lying cross-legged recumbent on a green shaped scrolled base and, right, a similar dog with grey patches. 3⅝in. long. c.1835–50. This model comes from the factory responsible for the animals appearing in Colour Plates 96 and 147.*

The pair of greyhounds shown in Colour Plate 16 are remarkably similar to the pair of Copeland & Garrett dogs appearing in Colour Plate 7. However, a close examination reveals small differences in the modelling. They are unmarked, as is also the further example illustrated in Colour Plate 17. Whether the factory responsible, whatever its identity, copied the Copeland & Garrett dogs or vice versa, it is impossible to say.

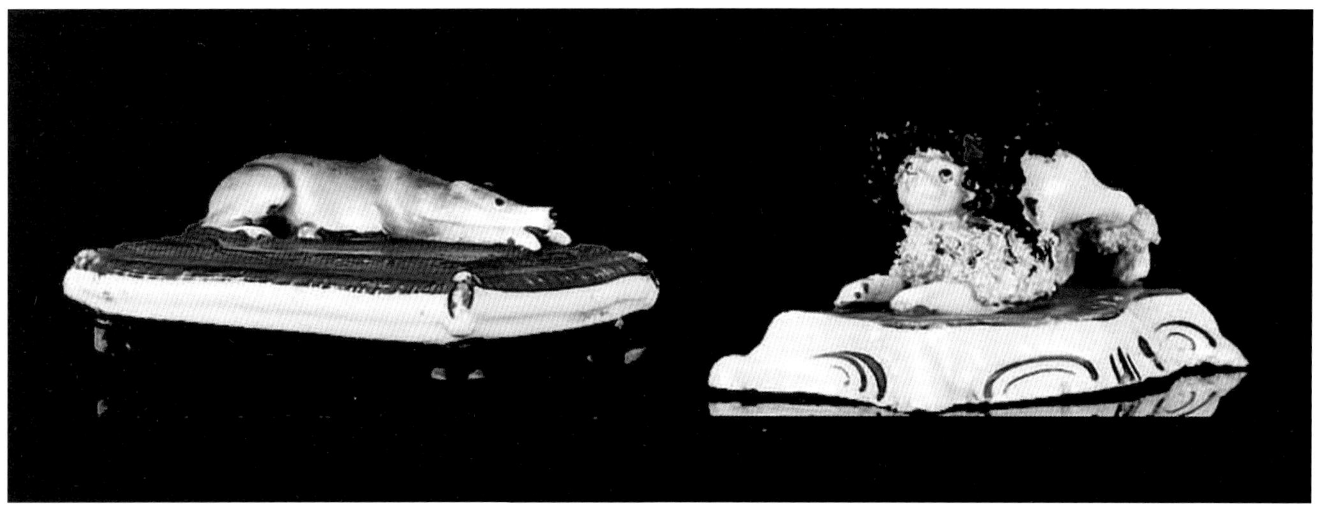

COLOUR PLATE 19.
a (left). *Staffordshire greyhound recumbent on a puce and white rectangular base with tassels, supported by four bun feet. 3¼in. long. c.1835–50.*
b. (right). Staffordshire parti-coloured poodle lying recumbent with hindquarters raised, on a green shaped rectangular base moulded with scrolls. 3½in. long. c.1835–50. For another example of this model see Colour Plate 96.
Christie's South Kensington

PUGS

Pugs, which seem to have originated in China, were brought over to this country from Holland by William and Mary in 1688, and hence were initially called 'Dutch dogs'. They were popular throughout Europe in the eighteenth century, being, incidentally the badge or symbol of Mopsorden or the Order of the Pug (an institution that replaced the Order of Freemasons, membership of which was forbidden by the Pope in 1736 on pain of excommunication). Not surprisingly, pugs were produced in porcelain in considerable quantities by Meissen and other Continental factories. They were also made in this country during the eighteenth century at Chelsea, Bow, Derby and elsewhere. However, it is clear from Bewick's *A General History of Quadrupeds*, first published 1790, that they were growing out of favour by the end of the eighteenth century. Why this should have been is not altogether clear. A pug bitch and her puppy from a drawing by Philip Reinagle are illustrated in *The Sportsman's Cabinet,* published in 1803, and the comments made by its author, William Taplin, may have done something to accelerate the breed's decline:

> . . . in the whole catalogue of the canine species, there is not one of less utility, or possessing less powers of attraction than the pug dog . . . applicable to no support, appropriated to no useful purpose, susceptible of no predominant passion, and in no way whatever remarkable for any extra emminence [*sic*], he is continued from era to era for what alone he might have been originally intended, the patient follower of a ruminating philosopher, or the adulating and consolatory companion of an old maid.

Whatever the reason for the decline in the pug's popularity, the breed seems to have fallen completely out of favour at least by 1830. Save in connection with ear-cropping, pugs were not even mentioned by William Youatt in his book *The Dog*, and this fall from grace is reflected in the disappearance of porcelain models from shortly after 1830 till much later in the century,[27] to be replaced by King Charles spaniels. I say King Charles spaniels rather than poodles, because there is evidence that prior to 1830 poodles were produced concurrently with pugs.

Certainly, the real dogs existed side by side as lap-dogs, as is clear from the following passage from Charlotte Brontë's *Shirley*, written in 1848/9 but set in the latter part of the Napoleonic Wars (1803–15). The conversation is between one of the local curates and the heroine, Shirley (Miss Keeldar):

> 'A very dangerous dog that, Miss Keeldar. I wonder you should keep such an animal'.
> 'Do you Mr. Donne? Perhaps you will wonder more when I tell you I am very fond of him'.
> 'I should say you are not serious in the assertion. Can't fancy a lady fond of that brute [it had a bulldog element in its ancestry], 'tis so ugly – a mere carter's dog. Pray hang him'.
> 'Hang what I am fond of!'
> 'And purchase in his stead some sweetly pooty pug[28] or poodle – something appropriate to the fair sex. Ladies generally like lap dogs'.

Unlike poodles, King Charles spaniels, do not appear to have been manufactured to any significant extent before about 1830, but thereafter were turned out on an ever-increasing scale.

However, during the first thirty years of the nineteenth century interest in the pug was still sufficiently strong to ensure that the breed was well represented in porcelain in this country. The modern reader will be struck by the difference in shape between the pug of the nineteenth century and the pug of today, the proportions being quite different. The earlier version stood higher, was smaller in the skull, lighter in the bone, longer in the muzzle, and not so wide in the front. Pugs of the period with which we are concerned are usually fawn.[29] From time to time black puppies were thrown up in a litter, but they were normally drowned at birth, being regarded as unlucky. Indeed black pugs were not taken seriously by breeders until about 1886, although twenty years earlier Lady Brasey had exhibited one at the Maidstone show; it was only after 1918 that outstanding black pugs were bred.

An interesting feature of pugs produced in this country during the eighteenth and nineteenth centuries, with the exception of the Chelsea model of Hogarth's Trump,[30] is that the ears are cropped. The bitch and puppy appearing in *The Sportsman's Cabinet* (after Reinagle) referred to above have suffered this form of mutilation, and the porcelain animals merely reflected the treatment undergone by the real animals. Why pug dogs should have been mutilated in this way is not immediately obvious.

The motive for cropping is to prevent a fighting dog, for instance a bulldog or mastiff, being taken by the ears by its opponent, but as the pug was only a lap-dog, never a fighting dog, the need for cropping never existed. Sad to say, the malpractice would seem to have been simply in deference to the dictates of fashion. William Youatt denounced the malpractice observing: 'Mr. Blaine very naturally observes that it is not a little surprising that this cruel custom is so frequently, or almost invariably, practised on pug dogs, whose ears, if left alone, are particularly handsome and hang very gracefully'.[31]

Ear cropping, in addition to being practised on pugs, was also sometimes practised on Great Danes, Dalmatians and several varieties of terrier, seemingly in each case for reasons of fashion. Bull terriers were subjected to this form of mutilation even after baiting had been declared illegal in 1835, and, again, the justification must have been simply fashion. However, in 1895 the practice, which had previously been technically illegal, was accepted by the Kennel Club as unlawful, and dogs with cropped ears were banned from shows. Queen Victoria would not countenance any form of mutilation of her own dogs. Edward VII, when Prince of Wales, wrote to the Kennel Club expressing his disapproval of ear cropping and this doubtless helped to induce the Kennel Club to act in 1895.

Rockingham

The Rockingham factory turned out a pair of pugs, a dog and a bitch (in reverse) in two different versions. Examples of the earlier version (where the animal's rear does not quite touch the base, and the collar is without bells) are shown in Colour Plate 20. They consist of two dogs and a bitch. None of them is numbered, but the bitch has a painted Griffin mark indicating that it was a very early production. Presumably, the model came into existence before the beginning of the numbering system, and was never subsequently brought into it. The later version (which is a particularly close copy of the Derby pug modelled by Coffee[32]) is incised under the base 'No 76'. This model appears, as does the Derby equivalent, in three approximate sizes, namely 3¼in., 2⅝in. and 2⅛in. Sizes 2 and 3 are illustrated in Colour Plate 21.[33] Why the smaller dog should be incised to indicate its size with '2' instead of '3' is a mystery.

Whereas the pugs of Colour Plate 21 are dogs, the pug shown in Colour Plate 22a is a

COLOUR PLATE 20. *Two fawn-coloured Rockingham pug dogs, each seated on an oval maroon base moulded with white and gilt scrolls; in the centre, a Rockingham pug bitch in white and gold seated on a similarly shaped white and gilt scroll base, the dogs 2⅝in. high, the bitch 2½in. high. Unnumbered. 'Cl. 2' under the bases of the dogs, the red Griffin mark under the base of the bitch. 1826–30.*

bitch. Bitches are rarer than dogs. An interesting feature of the bitch of Colour Plate 22a is that it is not the reverse of the dogs shown in Colour Plate 21. However, dogs of this model are recorded as pairs in reverse, and presumably the bitch was paired with a dog in reverse.

Why the Rockingham factory should have abandoned the original pug design in favour of the later version,[34] which, when all is said and done, is not all that different, is somewhat puzzling. However, since in the case of the earlier model the animal's rear is slightly above the base, that particular model must have been more difficult to make, and presumably the factory chose to adopt the simpler form of construction where the dog sits firmly on the base.

The Rockingham factory also produced a begging pug, slightly tubby in form; it stands on a polygon base. The only example known to the author is illustrated in Colour Plate

COLOUR PLATE 21. *Two fawn-coloured Rockingham pugs, one 2⅝in. high, seated on a green, the other 2⅛in. high on a maroon, oval base moulded with white and gilt scrolls. Incised 'No 76., Cl. 2. Impressed mark. The smaller dog is incised '2'. 1826–30.*

Colour Plate 22.
a. (left). Fawn-coloured Rockingham pug bitch seated on a green oval base moulded with white and gilt scrolls. 2⅞in. high. Incised 'No 76'. Cl. 2. 1826–30.
b. (right). Derby fawn-coloured pug bitch seated on a green oval scroll base with a touch of turquoise 2¼in. high. c.1830.

23b. It carries under the base the impressed mark and a 'Cl. 2' in red, and is incised 'No 121'. Note the rich gilt band that edges the crimson base. Presumably, the late number indicates that the model came into existence towards the end of the factory's animal production, which would account for the model's rarity. There would simply have been insufficient time for many examples to have been manufactured. Moreover, such specimens as were produced must have been exposed to the risk of destruction. The distribution of weight consequent on the begging pose necessarily put the piece at risk of being knocked over. The pug of Colour Plate 23b is from its detailed modelling very much a dog, and this suggests that it had a bitch in reverse as its companion. No example has, however, so far emerged.

The white and gilt begging pug illustrated in Colour Plate 23a may also be from the Rockingham factory. For the paste and structure of the base (closed-in except for a centrally located hole) are consistent with a Rockingham attribution. They are, however, also consistent with a Derby origin. What favours a Rockingham provenance is the fact that the underside of the base is incised 'No 75', a number which immediately precedes that of the undoubted Rockingham pug model in a sitting position incised 'No 76'. Moreover no other Rockingham figure has been discovered with the number '75'. The difficulty is that I am not satisfied, from the manner in which 'No 75' has been incised, that the numbering is contemporaneous with the date of the pug's manufacture. And if the number was added later, it is more likely that the pug, since it would have been issued without a number, is a Derby product, which someone later sought to pass off as Rockingham. On this basis, was the selection of 'No 75', rather than some other number, simply the result of realisation on the part of the person adding the number that 'No 75' would conveniently fill a vacancy in the Rockingham figure series and would immediately precede in the numbering sequence an undoubted Rockingham pug model in a different pose? Or did he arrive at the number from seeing a genuine Rockingham pug of the same shape and size incised 'No 75'? If the latter was the case, then figure 'No 75' is, in the Rockingham figure series, indeed a begging pug, albeit the pug illustrated in Colour Plate 23a is not an example of such a pug. If the white and gilt pug of Colour Plate 23a is not from the Rockingham factory it must have a Derby origin.

COLOUR PLATE 23.
a. (left). Derby or Rockingham white and gilt begging pug. 2¼in. high. c.1830.
b. (right). Rockingham fawn-coloured begging pug standing on a crimson polygon base. 2½in. high. Incised 'No 121'. Cl. 2. Impressed mark. 1826–30.

Derby (Nottingham Road)
Included in Haslem's list of unnumbered figures[35] are:

		Enamelled and Gilt	
Large Pug Dogs, per pair, Coffee		4s	0d
Less Ditto, ditto, ditto		3s	0d
Small Ditto, ditto, Coffee		2s	0d
Begging Pugs, ditto, Chelsea	2s	0d	

COLOUR PLATE 24.
Three Derby white and gilt pugs, each seated on an oval scroll base, two 2⅝in. high, incised under the base '2', the other 2¼in. high, incised '3', to indicate size. c.1830.

On the face of it, the last entry looks like a reference to a known eighteenth century model, but, be that as it may, nineteenth century examples undoubtedly exist. One of these models, naturistically coloured and wearing a gold collar, stands on a green mound base, 3in. high overall.[36] A begging pug also appears with a seated boy in model No 51.

The other pug models referred to by Haslem would also appear to be eighteenth century in origin, as they are attributed to Coffee, who began modelling circa 1794, and they are included in Bemrose's list of moulds, models, etc. belonging to William Duesbury in 1795: 'Pair large pug dogs, 3 sizes'. Derby pug dogs in various sizes go back to about 1758 and presumably Coffee produced up-to-date versions.

The nineteenth century Derby pugs appear, as in the case of Haslem's list, in three approximate sizes, namely 3¼/3in., 2⅝in. and 2¼in. high respectively, and those sizes are frequently designated in descending order by the numbers '1', '2' or '3' incised under the base.[37] Presumably these are the Coffee models carried over into the nineteenth century. Examples are shown in Colour Plates 24 and 26.

An interesting example, 2¼in. high, is seated on a green base edged with gilt scrolls. The noteworthy feature of this particular animal was that it carried the Bloor Derby mark under the base.[38] Another example, this time 3in. high, had an 'iron-red mark'. It is rare indeed for an example to be marked.[39]

Normally, coloured Derby pugs were fawn, but a rare black specimen (size 2), 2½in. high is shown in Colour Plate 26, demonstrating that real black pugs were occasionally preserved, and not all of them drowned at birth. It is interesting to note the appearance of 'A black pug dog 10s' in Christie's 'CATALOGUE of The Remainder of the Valuable Stock of the CHELSEA Porcelain Manufactory' sold on 5 May 1778. It should also be mentioned that nineteenth century pugs of the type discussed above are recorded in biscuit.

Colour Plate 25. *Pair of 'New' Derby fawn-coloured pugs, each seated on a green oval cushion on a rectangular stool edged with a continuous gilt line. 3¼in. high. Mark: Crown over crossed batons, dots and 'D' in red. '41' in red. Modelled by Edward Keys. c.1830.*

COLOUR PLATE 26. *Derby black pug seated on a green and turquoise oval scroll base. 2½in. high. Incised '2'. c.1830.*

Included among the models of Edward Keys are:

	Enamelled and gilt
New Sitting Pugs, on Cushions	1s 6d

The pair of Derby pugs illustrated in Colour Plate 25, each seated on a green cushion on a rectangular stool base, are the 'New Sitting Pugs, on Cushions' referred to. They are marked in red under the base with a Crown over crossed batons, dots and a 'D'. They are also inscribed in red '41'. That these pugs are the work of Edward Keys, and therefore the models referred to in the list of figures attributed to him, can be demonstrated by the head of the pugs, which is identical with that of Keys' monkey musicians[40] also included by Haslem among Edward Keys' work. As Keys modelled the monkey musicians, he must also have modelled the pugs of Colour Plate 25. The head of each pug is, of course, differently decorated from that of each monkey musician, so as to show the nature of the animal being represented, but a careful examination of the shape of the head will show that it is identical in each case.

Another pair of Derby pugs, similar to the above, but where the stool base was supported on four ball feet, appeared at the International Ceramics Fair London, 1991. One was a dog, the other a bitch. They were each 3½in. high.

For completeness, it should be mentioned that a well-known Derby eighteenth century model in the form of a stocky pug with a collar fitted with round metal balls seated erect on a rectangular base, 3½in. high,[41] was continued into the nineteenth century and examples are occasionally to be found. A smaller version, 2in. high, is also recorded.

Colour Plate 27.
White-glazed standing pug from the King Street factory, Derby. Sampson Hancock mark in blue. 2in. long. Later nineteenth century.

Derby (King Street)
Shown here are a white-glazed standing pug (Colour Plate 27), a white glazed seated pug (Colour Plate 28) and a white glazed group of three pugs (Colour Plate 29). In each case the Sampson Hancock mark in blue appears.

Colour Plate 28.
White-glazed seated pug from the King Street factory, Derby. Sampson Hancock mark in blue. 6in. long. Later nineteenth century.

Colour Plate 29.
White-glazed group from the King Street factory, Derby consisting of three pugs, with heavily studded collars, on a deep irregular base. Sampson Hancock mark in blue. 7in. long. Later nineteenth century.

Chamberlain Worcester

The Chamberlain factory produced a pair of pug models, one the reverse of the other, each seated on a rectangular base with rounded corners (Colour Plates 31, 32, and 33 top row).[42] The factory also turned out another model (Colour Plate 30b) seated on a cushion base with tassels, and this was presumably executed in pairs.

It is interesting to note that a collection of animals sent in December 1816 from the factory to the London shop included '2 Pugs'. Pug dogs appear to have been among the

Colour Plate 30.
a. (left). Charles Bourne fawn-coloured pug seated on a dry-blue cushion with gilt tassels, inscribed under the base in red '7'. 2⅝in. high. 1817–30.
b. (right). Chamberlain Worcester pug seated on a dry-blue cushion base with gilt tassels. 2⅝in. high. c.1820–40.

Colour Plate 31. *Chamberlain Worcester fawn-coloured pug seated on a green rectangular base with rounded corners. Mark: 'Chamberlain Worcester' written in red script. 2½in. high. c.1820–40.*

Colour Plate 32. *Chamberlain Worcester fawn-coloured pug seated on a green rectangular base with rounded corners. 2⅝in. high. Mark 'Chamberlains Worcester' written in script. c.1820–40. This is the reverse model of the pug of Colour Plate 31.* Phillips

earliest animals produced by the Chamberlain concern. For there is a reference[43] in the factory documents of November 1802 to '8 Pug doggs, coloured proper at 3s 0d'.

Seemingly of about that date is the group illustrated in Mortlock Ltd.'s advertisement.[44] It consists of a seated pug with left front paw upraised and a recumbent puppy beside it. A particularly interesting feature is the absence of any base. Freestanding models of animals of the first half of the nineteenth century are very rare.

Pugs must have continued at the Chamberlain factory up to at least 1829. For in a document of that date there is mention[45] of 'A pug dog 2s 6d'.

Grainger Lee & Co., Worcester

No pug dog has been recorded as emanating from the Grainger Lee factory, nor does such an animal appear in the factory pattern book. However, not all the factory's animals are to be found in that book, so that it is not impossible that a Grainger Lee pug will one day come to light.

Royal Worcester

The researches of Henry Sandon, based on the factory records, have revealed that in 1862 the Royal Worcester factory modelled a group of pugs (item 109 in the factory list), in 1872 a pug seated (item 267) and a pug standing (item 268), in 1873 a life-size pug standing (item 355),[46] and in 1875 a pug bitch (item 506).

COLOUR PLATE 33. *Top row. Chamberlain Worcester pug seated on a dry-blue rectangular base with rounded corners. 2¾in. high. Red script mark. c.1820–40.*
Second row (left). Minton pug lying recumbent on a claret cushion base with yellow tassels. 4in. long. c.1831–40.
Second row (right). Minton greyhound recumbent on a green cushion base with yellow tassels. 4in. long. c.1831–40. Compare this greyhound with that of Colour Plate 4.
Third row (left). Minton fawn-coloured pug recumbent on a claret base, rectangular with rounded corners. 3¼in. long. c.1831–40.
Third row (right). Minton fawn-coloured pug recumbent on a blue base, rectangular with rounded corners. 3¼in. long. c.1831–40. Christie's South Kensington

Minton

The Minton factory produced a pug lying recumbent on a tasselled cushion. It corresponds with illustration No 20 in the factory drawing book. Examples of this model appear in biscuit, white and gilt (Colour Plate 34), and in colour (Colour Plate 33 second row left). Sometimes the factory substituted a simpler base, rectangular in

COLOUR PLATE 34.
Minton pug, with blue and gilt collar, lying on a cushion base with gilt tassels. 4¼in. long. c.1831–40.

COLOUR PLATE 35.
Minton fawn-coloured pug with black features and black and gilt collar, lying on a rectangular gilt-banded base with rounded corners. 3¾in. long. c.1831–40.

form with rounded corners (Colour Plates 33, third row, and 35).

The Minton pug also appears as part of a paperweight, in the same way as does the Minton spaniel of Figure 12. An example of a pug paperweight was to be seen at the London Ceramics Fair in June 1992 where the extended base was not encrusted with flowers, but instead painted with scenes.

Two interesting pugs, naturistically coloured, each seated on a liver-red mound base

COLOUR PLATE 36. *Samuel Alcock group of a standing fawn pug with black collar and a seated King Charles spaniel with black spots on a pale yellow scrolled mound base. 3¼in. long. Impressed '342'. c.1840–50.*
Christie's South Kensington

edged with gold and closed in underneath save for a centrally located hole, 2¾in. high overall, appeared in a sale in January 1997 together with a plain white example on a puce base.[47] The colour of the bases suggest a Minton rather than a Derby origin. Unfortunately, a pug of this shape, does not appear anywhere in the factory drawing book, but it could be one of the models there numbered, but not described or illustrated.

Samuel Alcock

Pugs do not feature significantly in the output of the Samuel Alcock factory. It may be that, by the time the factory came to manufacture animals on any scale, the pug dog had fallen out of favour, and the management considered that it was not worthwhile producing replicas of this particular breed to any significant extent. There are, however, two Samuel Alcock groups which include a pug. In the one case a pug is modelled standing together with a seated King Charles spaniel on a mound base impressed '342' (Colour Plate 36) The second Alcock group featuring a pug can be seen in

COLOUR PLATE 37. *Samuel Alcock group consisting of a brown-spotted pug confronting on yellow steps a black-spotted cat with ears and back arched, all on a flat green rectangular base with canted corners. 2¾in. high. Impressed '266'. c.1840–50.*

COLOUR PLATE 38. *Another example of the model shown in Colour Plate 37.*
Christie's South Kensington

Colour Plate 37. The dog is modelled confronting a cat with ears laid back and back arched standing on steps.

Charles Bourne

An example of a Charles Bourne pug is illustrated in Colour Plate 30a. It is easily confused with the Chamberlain Worcester version (Colour Plate 30b).

COLOUR PLATE 39. *Staffordshire group of a pug bitch crouching on a green stool (standing on a green plinth base), three puppies playing beneath, the animals eccentrically painted in tan and dark brown. 3⅞in. long. c.1835–50.*
Christie's South Kensington

Unidentified Staffordshire Factories

The view conjecturally attributed above to the Samuel Alcock factory on the marketability of a pug, at least as an independent model, may have been shared by the unidentified Staffordshire factories operating at this time. For Staffordshire pugs are but rarely encountered; the King Charles spaniel had taken over.

The two pug dogs illustrated in Colour Plate 40 are not, as one might at first sight

COLOUR PLATE 40. *Pair of Staffordshire pugs, each seated on a green base. 2½in. high. c.1830. Note the similarity to the Derby version (in Colour Plates 24 and 26)* John Read Antiques

think, from the Derby factory, though the modelling seems largely indistinguishable from that of the pugs of the latter concern (see, for example, Colour Plate 24). However, they do not have the same quality as Derby pugs, and the underneath of the bases is different. Instead of being closed in, except for a centrally located hole, they are recessed. These animals must come from somewhere in Staffordshire, but from a factory of distinction which would seem to have made a blatant copy of the Derby version.

Another rare Staffordshire pug dog is illustrated in colour Plate 41.

COLOUR PLATE 41. *Staffordshire pug seated on a cobalt-blue mound base edged with a continuous gilt line. 2⅞in. high. c.1835–50.*
Christie's South Kensington

POODLES

The poodle originated in either France or Germany – which is a matter of dispute – and is found in all parts of the Continent and even further afield. It is a dog of considerable antiquity, being mentioned by Gessner in 1524. To begin with, it was employed as a gun-dog for duck shooting and was called a 'water dog' or 'rough water dog'. What is clearly an unclipped poodle and referred to as a 'water dog' is illustrated in William Taplin's *The Sportsman's Cabinet* published in 1803. It is there distinguished from the water spaniel. A similar animal, likewise unclipped and there called the 'large rough water dog', appears in Thomas Bewick's *A General History of Quadrupeds* first published in 1790. However, notwithstanding these illustrations, the poodle was normally trimmed with what came to be known as the 'lion-clip'. Interestingly, a print entitled 'The Dog Barbers', published by Bretherton in 1771, shows poodles in France being clipped. A later print dated 1819 depicts two Frenchwomen energetically clipping poodles with enormous scissors on the Pont Neuf in Paris, and a traveller's diary entry of 1821 interestingly contains the comment 'We crossed the Seine by the Pont Royal . . . on the bridge were several women clipping poodles'.[48] The reason for subjecting the animal to the lion-clip was to enable it, when it was being used for retrieving duck, to shake off the water as it emerged. The area of its body which contained the vital organs or which might be susceptible to rheumatism, for example the knees, were protected by leaving the hair untrimmed.

However, it would seem that before the lion-clip came to be adopted, shaving was more extensive. Thus, in the painting 'Wild Duck Aroused' by J.B. Oudry (1686–1755),[49] the poodle depicted, with fierce expression, chasing duck, does not have the lion-clip but, except for the head and the end of the tail, is shaved completely. In view of the date of the painting, presumably the more extensive shaving represented the original practice, and the lion-clip was adopted later. This view is confirmed by the same essential treatment given to

COLOUR PLATE 42. *Two Chelsea poodles in begging pose on mound bases, with gold anchor marks. 3⅝in. high. c.1765.*
Christie's South Kensington

the poodle, the head and neck alone remaining unclipped, appearing in a portrait of William, 1st Baron Russell of Thornhaugh (1553–1613) father of the 4th Earl Bedford.[50] The painting is dated 1588; interestingly, the poodle had arrived in England by at least 1588.

Although the lion-clip seems to have replaced the more extensive shaving of earlier times, the latter practice would seem not to have been abandoned altogether. For the dogs of Colour Plates 55 and 56, presumably representing dogs of the time, are shaved all over except for the head and the ankles.

Although poodles started off as gun-dogs, soon many of them became pets. Thus, a mezzotint of 1780 by Sayer & Bennet from a series entitled 'Jack on a Cruise', shows a sailor trying to attract the attention of a young lady, accompanied by a small gambolling poodle trimmed with the traditional lion-clip. An unclipped poodle as a lap-dog appears in the painting of 'Nellie O'Brien' by Joshua Reynolds (1723–92).[51] By the beginning of the nineteenth century, and throughout it, the poodle had in this country come to be predominantly a pet, and not a gun-dog. However, its popularity seems not to have really taken off until after about 1830. It was only after that date that porcelain replicas came to be produced in quantity.

It should also be mentioned that poodles are remarkably intelligent and, as a result, had from the beginning always been regular performers in various forms of entertainment. In 1700 a troupe of poodles, in an act called 'The Ball of Little Dogs', performed before Queen Anne. Somewhat later, in the eighteenth century, a troupe of some eighty miniature poodles performed a unique act, in which they sat at a banquet and were waited upon by other dogs of inferior breed. In 1750, twelve years before she ascended the throne, Catherine the Great of Russia was given a poodle by her husband Grand Duke Peter. The dog walked most of the time on its hind legs like a human, and was exceptionally playful, drawing to itself the admiring attentions of the ladies of the Court. It was allowed to sit at the table with a napkin round its neck, and it ate from its plate cleanly. Moreover, it would turn to the servant who stood behind it and with a yap would indicate that it wanted a drink.

Colour Plate 43. *Two white and gilt Rockingham poodles, each seated on a mound base. 3in. high. Both incised 'No 97', one also with the 'Cl.1' mark. 1826–30.*

During the nineteenth century poodles regularly appeared throughout England and Scotland as entertainers, jumping through hoops, dancing, performing somersaults and undertaking all manner of tricks. Doubtless it was their entertainment qualities, which contributed to their popularity among the public at large.

Normally, poodles appear in paintings as white, but instances are recorded where they are depicted parti-coloured (e.g. Richard Ramsey Reinagle's 'Poodle and Wildcat', 1793[52]) or even black (e.g. James Ward's 'Buff', 1812[53]), presumably reflecting the occasional appearance of real dogs of these colours.

Unlike pugs, poodles do not feature to any significant extent in eighteenth century English porcelain. An exception is the Chelsea model shown in Colour Plate 42, which is of course very rare. It was only in the nineteenth century that poodles in English porcelain came into their own.

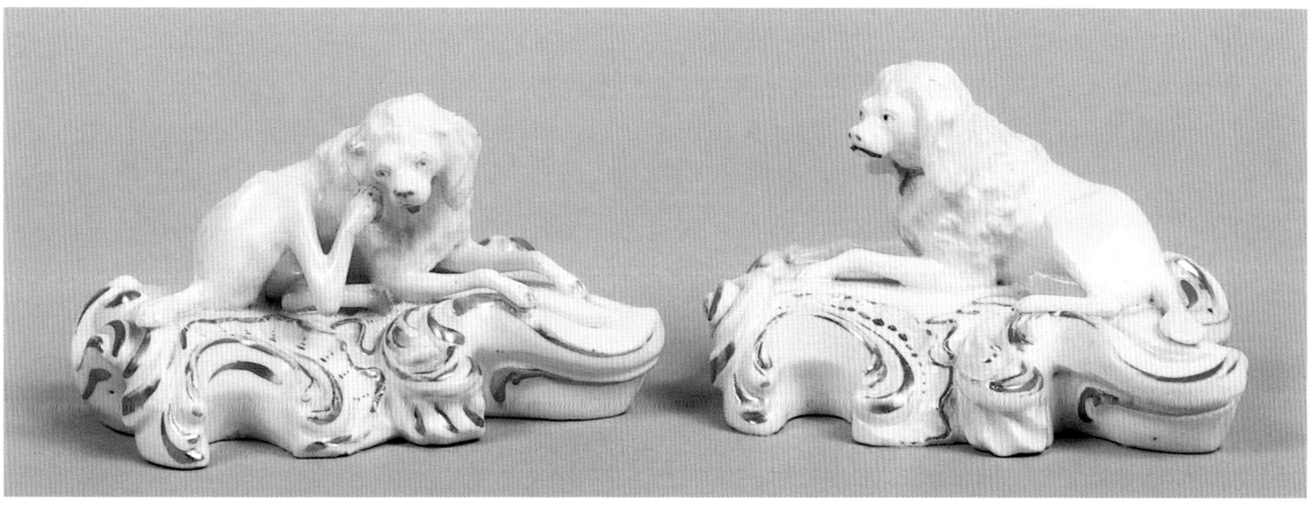

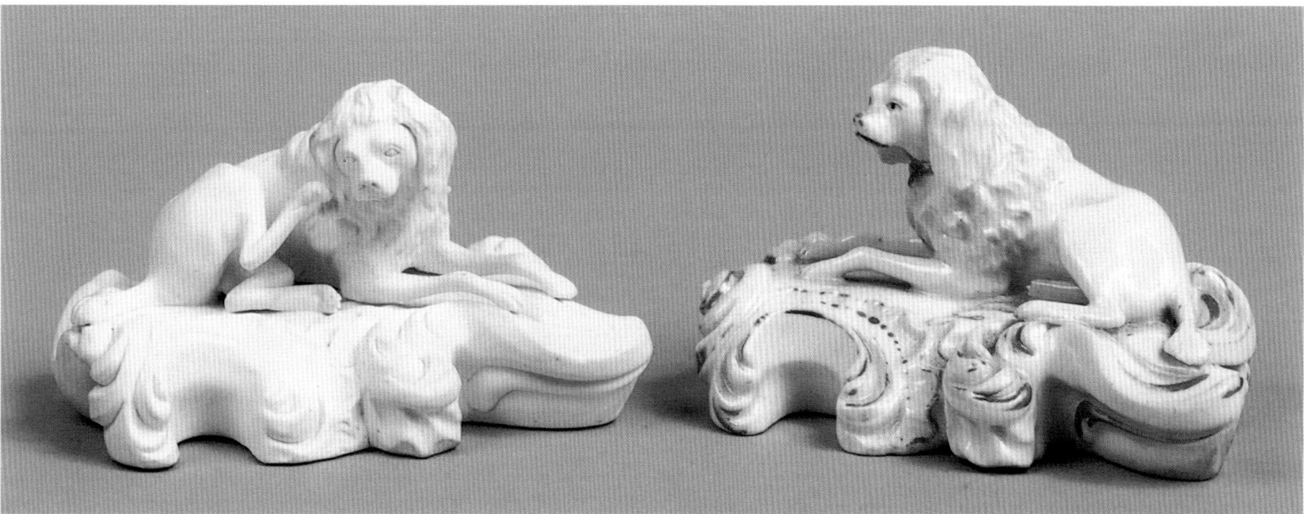

COLOUR PLATE 44. *Pair of Derby white and gilt poodles, the dog scratching, the bitch adopting a more dignified pose, each lying recumbent on a deep elaborately scrolled base. 4½in. long. Marked Crown over 'D' in red. c.1825–45.*

COLOUR PLATE 45. *a. (left). Derby biscuit poodle, scratching, lying recumbent on a deep elaborately scrolled base. 4in. long. c.1825–45.*
b. (right). Derby white and gilt poodle, companion model. 4in. long. Marked. Crown over 'D' in red. c.1825–45.

Rockingham

In view of the fact that the Rockingham factory was for many years best known to the public for the numerous poodles erroneously attributed to it, it is ironic that it was not until February 1988 that an example came to light which could properly be identified with the factory. Since then a further specimen (with a 'Cl. Mark') has appeared, the number of which, incised under the base, is, unlike that of the earlier discovered poodle, quite easy to read. The animal is incised 'No 97' and with the benefit of this knowledge careful scrutiny of the incised number of the other example shows it to be the same.[54] The two dogs are illustrated together in Colour Plate 43.[55] The model was also produced in reverse.[56]

Derby

There are two references by Haslem to Derby poodles.[57] They appear in his list of so-called 'Bow and Chelsea models':

	Enamelled and gilt	Biscuit
Poodle Dogs and Fleecy Sheep, each		5s 0d

And again in his list of models attributed to Edward Keys:

	Enamelled and gilt
New Poodle Dogs . . . each	2s 0d

The only undoubted Derby poodle models known to me appear in Colour Plates 44 and 45. The white and gilt examples that have survived unequivocally belong to the nineteenth century, because they have the contemporary 'Crown and 'D' mark' in red under the bases. But are they eighteenth century models carried over into the succeeding century? The elaborately scrolled rococo bases suggest that they are. They would seem to be the models referred to by Haslem under 'Bow and Chelsea models'. It is interesting to note that the prices given in the list relate solely to the biscuit, and a biscuit example of the dog scratching is illustrated in Colour Plate 45a. It is not possible to say for certain whether this particular example belongs to the eighteenth or nineteenth century, but judging by the paste, it is probably nineteenth century in origin.

It was not until about the middle of the 1820s that poodles came to be modelled to any significant extent by the various porcelain factories operating at the time. What more likely then that, when the animal came to be fashionable, and the inevitable subject of representation in porcelain by the Derby factory's competitors, the old eighteenth century version was resuscitated and reissued to satisfy demand? But the factory went further. It produced the 'New Poodle Dogs' appearing in the list of Edward Keys' models. Unfortunately, so far, examples of these 'New Poodle Dogs' have not come to light.

Illustrated in Colour Plate 50a is a toy poodle in biscuit, a mere 1¼in. high, with a flat closed-in base save for a centrally located hole. Doubtless it was made in the town of Derby, but whether it was turned out at the great Nottingham Road factory is problematical. Conceivably, it was a nineteenth century version of one of the:

	Enamelled and gilt
Begging French Dogs, per pair	2s 0d

appearing in Haslem's list of unnumbered models. But more likely, it was made by George Cocker or even Robert Blore, who for a short period operated as independent producers.

Chamberlain Worcester

What seems to have been the most popular basic poodle model produced at the Chamberlain Worcester factory is illustrated in Colour Plate 46. The dog, with an empty basket in its mouth, lies with its hind legs upraised on a tasselled cushion base. A variant is recorded where there is no basket and the dog is ridden by Cupid holding reins connected to the animal's mouth. The example illustrated in Colour Plate 47 is the same as that of Colour Plate 46 except for the rare substitution of pricked, or cropped, ears for those normally associated with poodles.[58]

The model of Colour Plate 46 also appears in enamel colours. A somewhat more elaborate version than usual – the dog reposed on a dry-blue cushion base with tassels and bows in addition – appeared at the Great Antiques Fair, Earls Court Exhibition 1997. The base was incised underneath with the factory mark including '155 Bond St.', the factory's London Showroom – normally the address is described as '155 *New* [my emphasis] Bond St.' – indicating that the piece must have been made no earlier than the

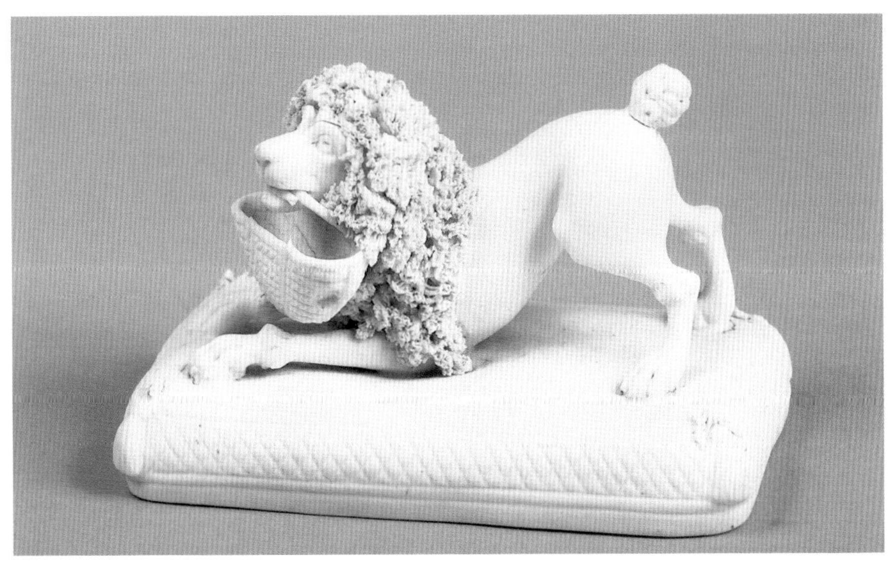

COLOUR PLATE 46. *Chamberlain Worcester poodle in biscuit lying on a tasselled cushion base with a basket in its mouth and with its hind legs upraised. 4in. long. Incised in script under the recessed base 'H Chamberlain and Sons Worcester'. c.1820–40.*

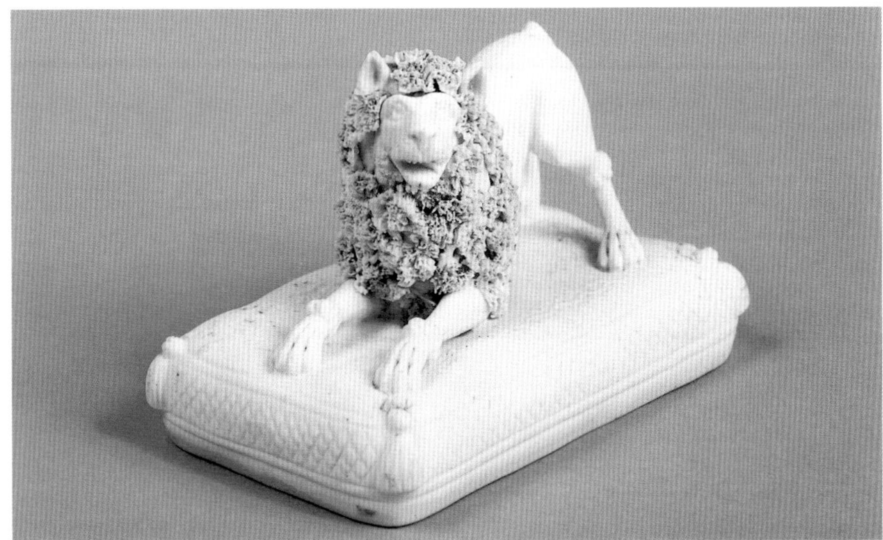

COLOUR PLATE 47. *Chamberlain poodle in biscuit with pricked ears and with hind legs upraised, lying on a tasselled cushion base. 4in. long. Inscribed in script under the recessed base 'Chamberlains Royal Porcelain Manufacturers'. c.1820–40. Note the cropped ears, an unusual feature in the case of poodles, but compare Figure 7 (p.50) and Colour Plate 61.*

COLOUR PLATE 48. *Chamberlain poodle with a basket in its mouth, lying with its hind legs upraised on a dark-green rectangular base with rounded corners. 3⅞in. long. Incised factory mark c.1820–40.*

COLOUR PLATE 49. *Chamberlain poodle with a basket in its mouth lying with its hind legs raised on a green rectangular base with rounded corners, the edges of the base with a tooled gilt border. 3⅞in. long. Incised 'Chamberlains Royal Porcelain Manufacturers Worcester'. c.1820–40.* Phillips

COLOUR PLATE 50. *a. (left). Derby toy poodle in biscuit begging. 1¼in. high. c.1830–45.*
b. (right). Chamberlain Worcester poodle in biscuit standing on a mound base. 2in. long. Impressed under a completely closed-in base 'CHAMBERLAINS'. c.1847–52.

opening of the showroom in 1816. Incidentally, models incised 'Chamberlain *Royal* [my emphasis] Porcelain Manufacturers' must have been made after 1820, as the factory did not receive the Royal Warrant until after the accession of George IV.

An important example of a variant of the basic model holds in its mouth a basket of fruit. It is lying recumbent on a blue tasselled cushion with the elaborate printed Royal Arms mark and the New Bond Street address under the base.[59]

Sometimes the basic model, instead of lying on a cushion base with tassels, lies on a rectangular base with rounded corners. Examples are shown in Colour Plate 48 and 49.[60]

COLOUR PLATE 51. *Chamberlain Worcester poodle, seated on a dry-blue base, rectangular with rounded corners. 2¾in. high. Mark 'Chamberlain Worcester' written in script. c.1820–40. The wool is represented by the moulding of the porcelain, and not, as, for example, in the case of the Chamberlain poodles of Colour Plates 46-50, by the application of thin threads or granules of porcelain.*

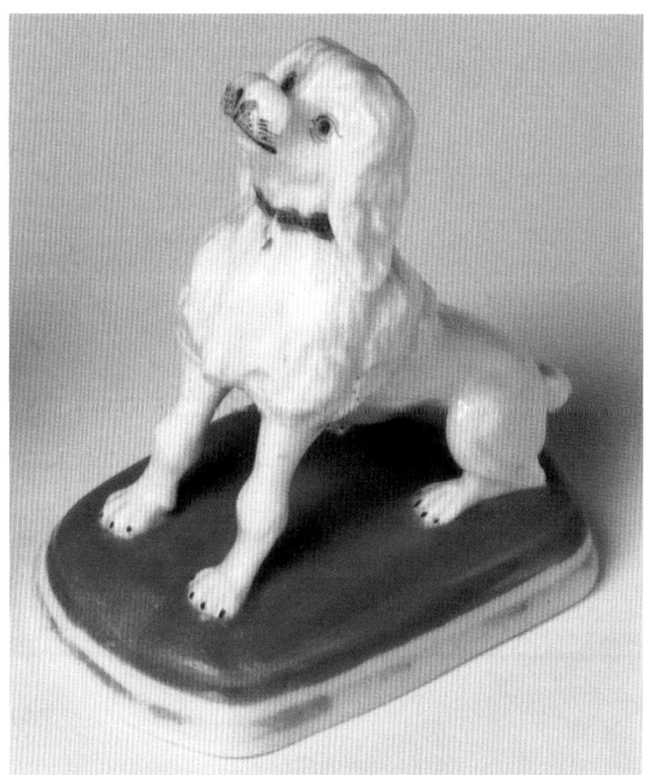

COLOUR PLATE 52. *Chamberlain Worcester poodle seated on a green rectangular base with rounded corners. 2¾in. high. Mark: 'Chamberlain Worcester' in red script. c.1820–40.* Phillips

Two completely different poodle models made at the Chamberlain Works are also recorded here. The first, seated upright on a dry-blue rectangular mound base with rounded corners, is shown in Colour Plate 51 (on a dry-blue base) and in Colour Plate 52 (on a green base).[61] Note the manner in which the wool is represented, i.e. by the moulding of the porcelain, and not by the application of threads of porcelain. The other model, which is really a toy,[62] is shown in Colour Plate 50b. It is clear from the mark that is was a late production.[63]

It is interesting to note that poodles are mentioned in the factory documents:[64]

2 New Poodles at	3s 0d [June 1824]
2 Poodles on blue cushions at	2s 6d
A toy biscuit poodle	5s 0d [September 1828]
To a biscuit poodle and shade	15s 0d [February 1829]

The price of the last item suggests that it was very large, a view supported by the reference to the preceding much cheaper biscuit poodle as a toy.

It is noteworthy that the Chamberlain, like the Derby, factory thought it expedient to produce *new* poodles and the documentary reference to them is June 1824. The 'new

COLOUR PLATE 53. *Grainger Lee poodle in biscuit with upraised hind legs, holding in its mouth a basket of flowers, on a cushion base with tassels. 4in. long. Impressed 'Grainger Lee & Co Worcester'. c.1820–37.*

poodles' modelled at Derby by Edward Keys must have come into existence between about 1821 (when he succeeded Isaac Farnsworth as Foreman) and 1826 (when he left the Derby factory). The Rockingham version was modelled in the period 1826–30. Which, if any, of the Chamberlain models here illustrated represents the 'new poodles' is unknown. Perhaps it will become clearer if and when the Derby 'New Poodle Dogs' come to light.

Grainger Lee & Co., Worcester

A poodle appears in the Grainger Lee drawing book belonging to the Dyson Perrins Museum, Worcester. The animal, with its hindquarters upraised, lies on a rectangular tasselled cushion supported by four bun feet. A porcelain example in biscuit is illustrated in Sandon.[65] It follows closely the design in the pattern book, the only slight deviation being that the tail is made to turn back on to the animal's body.

However, the factory also produced another version of a poodle, and this does not appear in the pattern book. The only known example, which, like the previous model mentioned, is in biscuit, is shown in Colour Plate 53. It has very great movement, and its upraised rear overhangs the tasselled cushion base. The stance is the same as that of the other poodle model, but this time the tail is quite different – it is short and terminates in a 'ball' of wool, and the cushion base no longer rests on four bun feet. If this was the later version, presumably these alterations were adopted to facilitate ease of manufacture. But the really interesting difference is that the poodle of Colour Plate 53 carries in its mouth a basket and, unlike the Chamberlain version (Colour Plate 46), a basket full of finely modelled flowers. Presumably, the addition of the basket of flowers was to enable the Grainger Lee poodle to rival the products of the Chamberlain and Minton factories, and the former factory could be a formidable competitor.[66]

COLOUR PLATE 54. *Minton poodle in biscuit lying recumbent on a cushion base with tassels. 4in. long. Model 'No 33'. c.1831–40. The basket, which should be in the animal's mouth, is, as is often the case, missing, only the handle remaining.*

Minton

The Minton factory produced two poodle models. They appear in the original drawing book as illustrations 19 and 33 respectively. The latter holds a basket in its mouth. The pose of both is similar to that of the Chamberlain model shown in Colour Plate 46. Each lies on a tasselled cushion, 4in. long.[67]

The biscuit poodle shown in Colour Plate 54 is an example of model No 33. Unfortunately, as is frequently the case with this model, the basket is missing, only the handle surviving in the dog's mouth. Collectors should be warned of the nefarious practice on the part of some dealers of converting such a surviving basket handle into a bone. The bone will, of course, be a fake, it never having been a feature of the model. The particular model illustrated in Colour Plate 54 is interesting for the fact that under the base are incised certain indistinct markings. It is possible, albeit with great difficulty and without any certainty, to read an incomplete date – '22 Feb 18'. If the reading is correct, it is frustrating in the extreme that the actual date year is missing. A fine pair of poodles (one the reverse) of model No 33 in biscuit were in the possession of Mercury Antiques Ltd. in 1986, still in their original glass display boxes.

Davenport

The base of the two well-modelled poodles of Colour Plate 55 bears a remarkable resemblance in shape to that of the King Charles spaniel of Colour Plate 131. It is rectangular with a raised centre and the same form of underneath construction. It is heavy in weight with some crazing. If the spaniel comes from the Davenport factory, it is conceivable the poodles do as well. However, the decoration is not as rich, and this is true of the same shaped poodle of Colour Plate 56b. Although the Davenport factory

COLOUR PLATE 55. *Two poodles with brown patches, each lying recumbent on an oval mound supported in turn by a rectangular base, one 2in. long. the other 1⅞in. Possibly Davenport. c.1830–50. Note the more extensive shaving than that of the 'lion-clip', see* *p.39–40.*

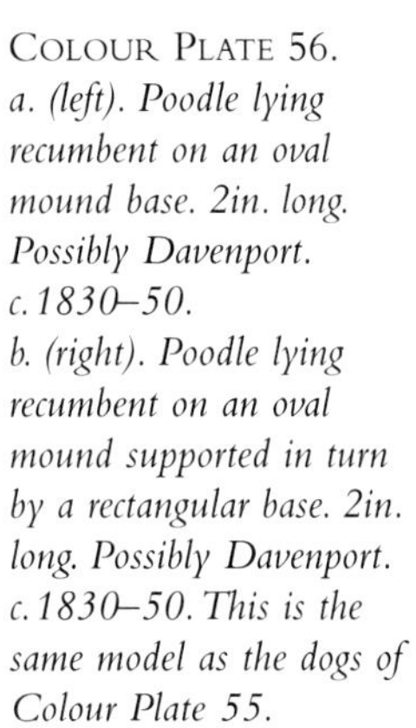

COLOUR PLATE 56.
a. (left). Poodle lying recumbent on an oval mound base. 2in. long. Possibly Davenport. c.1830–50.
b. (right). Poodle lying recumbent on an oval mound supported in turn by a rectangular base. 2in. long. Possibly Davenport. c.1830–50. This is the same model as the dogs of Colour Plate 55.

might possibly have turned out animals of different qualities, particularly if it was seeking to introduce its wares to the growing industrial population who might just be able to afford the cheapest animals, perhaps the more likely explanation is that some minor unknown Staffordshire factory was simply copying the finer model.

Samuel Alcock

One of the three animals buried under the foundation stone of the new Samuel Alcock factory opened in April 1839 was a poodle with upraised hindquarters. Only part of that particular example has survived, but a more satisfactory specimen is shown in Colour Plate 63a. Like the buried animal it has a bone in its mouth, and is impressed with the number '36'. A pair, each holding a bone, was exhibited at the Olympia Antiques Fair 1996. However, it would seem that sometimes, either accidentally or

COLOUR PLATE 57. *Pair of Samuel Alcock poodles, each seated on a heavily scrolled mound base in yellow. 3⅜in. high. Impressed '312'. c.1840–50.*

deliberately, the factory omitted to place the bone in the animal's mouth (Colour Plate 63b). The purpose may have been to produce a poodle barking.

The Samuel Alcock factory turned out various other poodle models (seemingly produced in pairs) namely, models numbered 7 (Colour Plate 61, Figure 7), 22 (Colour Plate 62), 95 (Colour Plate 64), 239 (with a cat, Colour Plate 68), 247 (Colour Plate 65[68]), 252 (Colour Plate 66), 311 (Colour Plate 67), 312 (Colour Plates 57, 58 and 59a)

COLOUR PLATE 58. *A further pair of Samuel Alcock poodles, each seated on a heavily scrolled mound base in yellow. 3⅜in. high. Impressed '312'. c.1840–50. There is a slight difference in the position of these dogs compared with the pair in Colour Plate 57.*

Colour Plate 59. a. *(left). Samuel Alcock poodle seated on a heavily scrolled mound base in yellow. 3⅞in. high. Impressed '312'. c.1840–50.*
b. (right). Samuel Alcock poodle seated very upright – more upright than the adjacent model – on a heavily scrolled mound base in yellow. 3⅝in. high. Unnumbered. c.1840–50. For a pair see Colour Plate 60.

COLOUR PLATE 60. *Pair of Samuel Alcock poodles, unnumbered – the same model as that of Colour Plate 59b. 3⅝in. high. c.1840–50.*

FIGURE 7. *Pair of unclipped Samuel Alcock poodles, with pricked ears, each standing on a green scrolled base edged with a gilt line. 2¼in. high. Number indecipherable, but this is model No 7. c.1835–50. For a coloured example see Colour Plate 61.* Sotheby's

COLOUR PLATE 61. *Samuel Alcock poodle with pricked ears, standing on a yellow rocky mound base. 2¾in. high. Impressed '7'. c.1835–50. For a pair see Figure 7.*

COLOUR PLATE 62. *Samuel Alcock poodle, holding in its mouth a yellow basket filled with green moss, and standing on a yellow scrolled base, rectangular in shape, with pinched-in sides. 2¾in. high. Impressed '22'. c.1835–50.*

and 323. No 323 consists of a dog clambering to eat out of a dish placed on what has been modelled as a pen-holder. In addition to the models mentioned above, there is an unnumbered model (Colour Plates 59b and 60). That this poodle comes from the Samuel Alcock factory is demonstrated beyond doubt by a comparison of the scrolled mouldings of the base with those of the two King Charles spaniels of Colour Plate 136. Interestingly, each of the three poodle examples illustrated here has a mark, ·/, in black under the base. Hopefully, it will be possible to ascertain the model number from other specimens (as and when they come to light) duly impressed with the appropriate numeral.

COLOUR PLATE 63.
a. (left). Samuel Alcock poodle with a bone in its mouth, lying recumbent with upraised hindquarters, on a scrolled mound base. 3¼in. long. Impressed '36'. c.1835–50.
b. (right). The same model in reverse with an open but empty mouth. There is nothing to indicate that this example ever had a bone.

COLOUR PLATE 64. *Pair of Samuel Alcock poodles, each recumbent with raised rear on a mound base, with a lump of meat or large bone in its mouth. 4¼in. long. Impressed '95'. c.1835–50.*
Oliver-Sutton Antiques

Mrs. Kate Villiers Clive illustrates[69] a group, on a rocky mound base edged with a thin, presumably gilt, line, which consists of a seated poodle, looking down at a recumbent cat 'pink with yellow markings', the two animals separated by a feeding bowl. The group looks like a product of the Samuel Alcock factory, but an attribution cannot safely be made.

It is to be noted that, in the case of models numbered 239, 247 and 252, the wool is represented by moulding, whereas in the other instances, it is represented by encrusted granules. Probably every model was produced after 1830, by which time the technique

COLOUR PLATE 65. *Samuel Alcock poodle standing on a yellow mound base. 3¼in. long. Impressed '247' c.1840–50.*
Oliver-Sutton Antiques

COLOUR PLATE 66. *Samuel Alcock poodle lying recumbent on a yellow mound base. 3½in. long. Impressed '252'.c.1840–50.*

COLOUR PLATE 67. *Samuel Alcock begging poodle, wearing a dunce's cap, on a yellow mound base. 4in. high. Impressed '311'. c.1840–50. This model is impressed with the same number as that appearing under the saluki in Colour Plate 214. As two different models could not carry the identical number, the factory clearly made a mistake (see p.139).*
Andrew Dando Antiques

of representing wool by encrusted granules was in vogue, but the Samuel Alcock factory did not invariably adopt that technique.

Charles Bourne

Recently a Charles Bourne poodle has come to light. It sits upright on a periwinkle-blue mound base, 2½in. high. The wool, which is subject to the lion-clip, is represented by moulding, not by encrusted granules. Under the base the number 11 appears in red.

COLOUR PLATE 68. *Samuel Alcock poodle and cat group on a light yellow mound base. 3½in. high. Impressed '239'. c.1840–50.*

COLOUR PLATE 69. *Lloyd Shelton poodle standing outside its white and gilt kennel on a green rocky rectangular base with rounded corners, encrusted with moss. 3⅛in. long. c.1835–45. Note the bowl of bones placed at the entrance of the straw-strewn kennel.*

Lloyd Shelton

The poodle of Colour Plate 69, though unmarked, probably emanates from the Lloyd Shelton factory. This attribution is founded on a similarity in shape and decoration to the base of a marked Lloyd Shelton figure.[70]

COLOUR PLATE 70. *Small Lloyd Shelton white poodle, with tail flicked back over its body, standing on a thin rectangular base edged with gold. 1⅝in. long. c.1835–45.*

COLOUR PLATE 71. *Lloyd Shelton white poodle with black markings on the muzzle, holding a black hat in its mouth and standing on a rectangular base with a continuous gilt line around the edge. 2¼in. long. c.1835–45.*

COLOUR PLATE 72. *a. (left). Lloyd Shelton poodle, with a basket of fruit in its mouth, standing on a rectangular base with rounded corners, edged on the front with gilt patterning. 7⅞in. high. c.1835–45. Beside it is a Staffordshire toy poodle with tail turned over standing on a rectangular base edged with a gilt band. 1⅝in. high, whose size is graphically illustrated by the 20p coin.*
b. (right). Detail of the basket of fruit in the dog's mouth.

A Lloyd Shelton attribution can still more confidently be given to the delightful toy white and gilt poodle illustrated in Colour Plate 70, notwithstanding that it too is unmarked. Apart from the quality of the gilding, a particular feature of the products of John and Rebecca Lloyd, identification with the Lloyd Shelton factory is unequivocally established by the appearance of the same poodle model on the base of the Lloyd Shelton figure of 'The Woodman'.[71] The thin white and gilt base of both the figure and also the independent model shown in Colour Plate 70 is substantially the same in form and decoration. Moreover the dog's tail turns back in a distinctive way in the case of both the animal that accompanies 'The Woodman' and the dog appearing in Colour Plate 70. The Lloyd Shelton model of 'The Woodman' is based on a Bartolozzi engraving after a print by Thomas Barker of Bath. Ironically the dog accompanying 'The Woodman' in the engraving would appear to be a lurcher; it is certainly not a poodle. Doubtless the factory found it more convenient to substitute the more fashionable breed. The same model as that shown in Colour Plate 70 appears in Colour Plate 71. The dog is somewhat larger, standing 2¼in. high overall. Interestingly it holds in its mouth a black hat of the shape worn by 'The Woodman'.

A further poodle model, this time a large one, standing 7⅞in. high with a basket in its mouth is attributed to the Lloyd Shelton factory. An example is shown in Colour Plate 72 together with a toy Staffordshire poodle and a 20p piece to demonstrate its size. By way of detail, the fruits in the basket are also shown.[72]

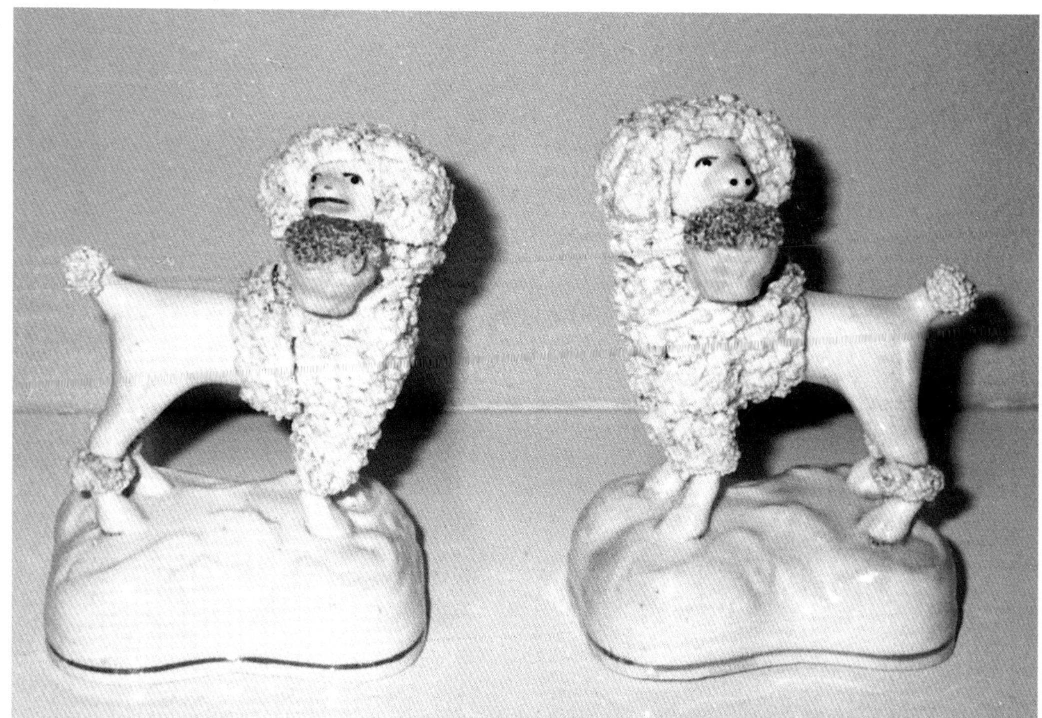

COLOUR PLATE 73. *Pair of Dudson poodles, each with a yellow basket in its mouth, standing on a scrolled base. 3¼in. high. c.1840–50.*

COLOUR PLATE 74. *Pair of Dudson poodle groups, each consisting of two poodles, one seated, the other recumbent, on a cobalt-blue shaped concave base. 2½in. long. c.1840–50.*

Dudson

The Dudson factory still exists, and Mrs. Audrey Dudson has carried out researches into its history. In the course of her investigations she has excavated the factory site, and discovered, among the wasters brought to light a quantity of shards which indicate the particular forms assumed by the animals produced by the factory in the 1840s. In reliance on these shapes, it is possible to attribute to the factory the poodles shown in Colour Plates 73 and 74.

COLOUR PLATE 75. *Two Staffordshire groups, each consisting of a boy with an unclipped poodle. 5½in. high. c.1840–50. Note the stream that runs down the base. The companion model in each case is a girl with a goat and kid.*

Unidentified Staffordshire Factories

Poodles were turned out in profusion during the period from 1830 to 1850 (particularly in the 1840s) and most of them came from the various unidentified Staffordshire factories operating at the time. These poodles exceeded in quantity any other breed of dog, although King Charles spaniels ran them close. Why poodles should have been so prolific is something of a mystery. Perhaps the real dogs assumed a unique popularity among the public, which was reflected in a corresponding demand for porcelain replicas. Perhaps interest in the breed was stimulated to an abnormal extent by the appearance of poodles at travelling circuses and other places of entertainment, which made them particularly appealing to children, and doubtless children were an important market.

The porcelain models of the period 1830–50 normally represent pet or circus dogs, not the sporting animals.[73] Sometimes they appear in comic pose, e.g. holding a black hat in their mouth (Colour Plates 93 and 112a) or being ridden by a monkey. Staffordshire poodles in different positions, e.g. lying recumbent (flat or with hindquarters raised), begging, standing or seated, sometimes with a basket in their mouth, sometimes not, are here illustrated. The animals themselves are normally white,

FIGURE 8. *Staffordshire black-spotted poodle seated on a tapering rectangular plinth with stiff leaf border between two gilt lines. 9½in. high. c.1830–40. Parti-colour poodles are rare.* Sotheby's

though their bases are often coloured. Occasionally, the animals are found parti-coloured (Figure 8, Colour Plate 96), and very rarely black (Colour Plate 98).

The group consisting of a poodle bitch and three puppies, which appears in Colour Plate 77 on a yellow cushion base with blue tassels, is also recorded on a blue cushion base with yellow tassels,[74] on a green cushion base with white and gilt tassels (Colour Plate 78), and in another instance in plain white. It would seem, incidentally, that the factory responsible was also responsible for the poodle and puppies group on the boxes shown in Colour Plate 76. One of these boxes, with its heavy crazing, looks more pottery than porcelain. It was clearly meant to be porcelain, but the mixture of which it was composed was clearly unsatisfactory, giving it a sub-standard appearance.

COLOUR PLATE 76. *Pair of Staffordshire flower-decorated boxes, with orange cushion lids, each surmounted by a poodle with puppies, one puppy missing from the right-hand example. 3½in. long. c.1840–50. The box on the right, heavily crazed, is possibly pottery.*

COLOUR PLATE 77. *Staffordshire poodle bitch with three puppies on a yellow cushion base with blue tassels. 3½in. long. c.1835–50*

COLOUR PLATE 78. *Staffordshire group of a poodle bitch with three puppies lying on a green cushion with white and gilt tassels (the lid to a box). 3⅝in. long. c.1835–50. (Compare with Colour Plate 79.)*

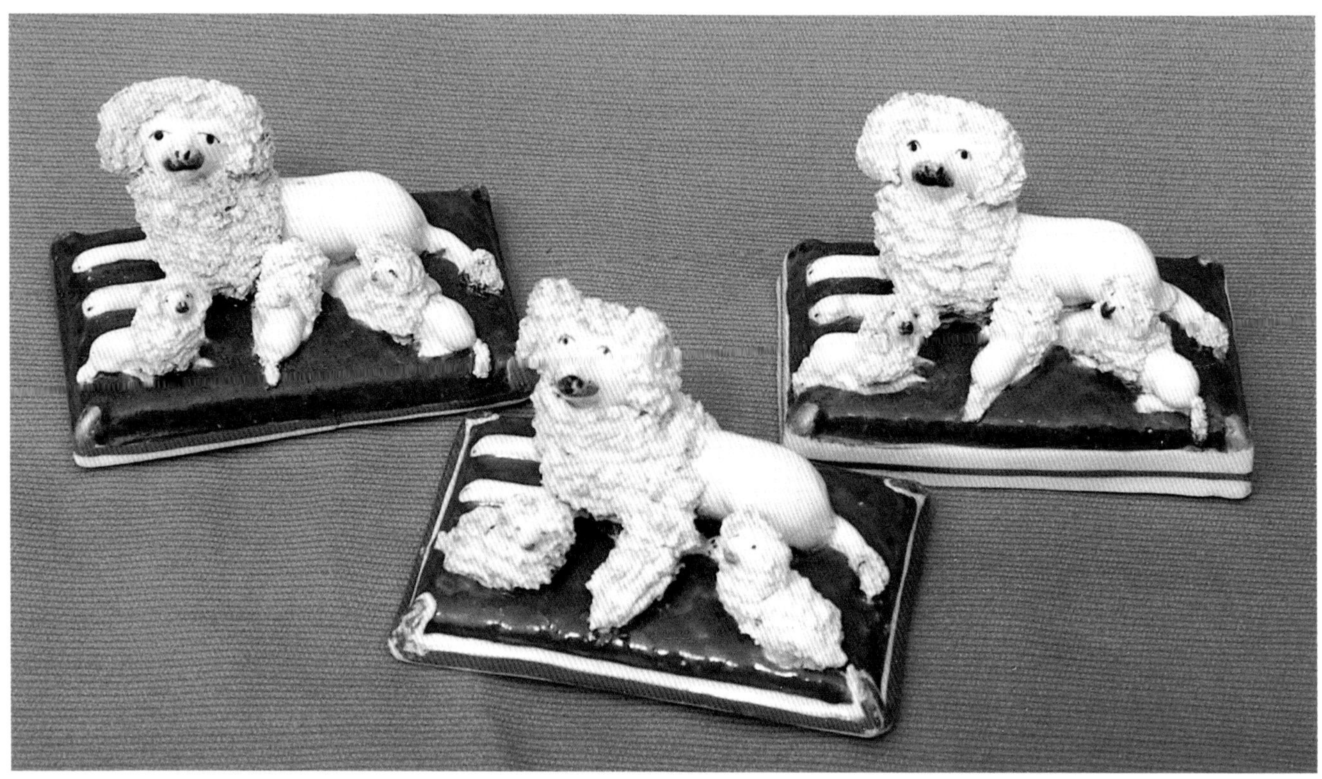

Colour Plate 79. *Three poodle and puppies groups, each on a green cushion base with gilt tassels, two of them lids. 3⅝in. long. c.1835–50.*

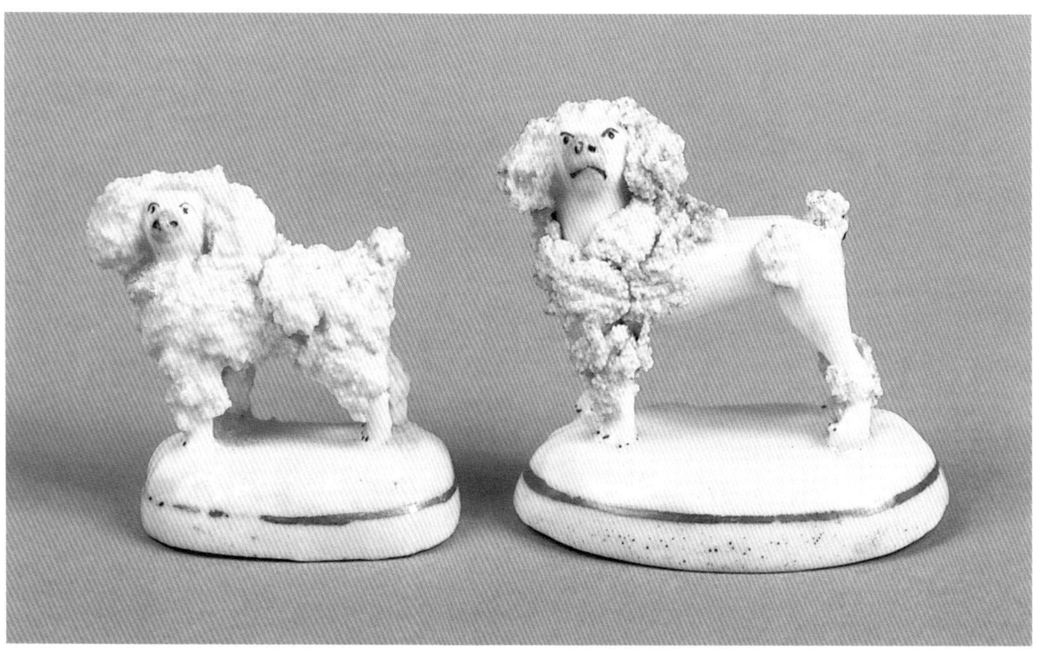

Colour Plate 80. *a. (left). Staffordshire toy poodle standing on an oval mound base edged with a continuous gilt line. 1¾in. high. c.1835–50.*
b. (right). Staffordshire toy poodle standing on an oval mound base edged with a continuous gilt line. 1⅞in. high. c.1835–50.

COLOUR PLATE 81. *Pair of Staffordshire toy poodles, each standing on a rectangular mound base edged with a gilt line. 1⅜in. high. In the centre a Staffordshire begging poodle on a round mound base edged with a gilt line. 1¾in. high. c.1835–50.*

The dog and three puppies on a green base with white and gilt tassels, illustrated in Colour Plate 78, is a box lid (as are two of the items in Colour Plate 79), and not an independent animal group. Whereas the same group on an orange base with gilt tassels, which forms the lids to the boxes shown in Colour Plate 76, has a simple continuous flange under the base to slot into the top of each box, the flange of the lid of Colour Plate 78 is shaped and non-continuous, clearly designed to lock into the matching box free of the danger of sliding off. Presumably it was a later version, modified in the interests of greater safety.

The poodles shown in Colour Plates 82, 84 and 85b (and possibly Colour Plate 83) would seem to have the same factory of origin. The colour most frequently used by that factory was pink. The bitch and puppies group of Colour Plate 83 appears in modified form where the puppy looking over the bitch's back is omitted. An example with a cobalt-blue base is recorded.[75] Incidentally, the use of cobalt blue indicates a post-1840 date of origin, and this helps to identify the age of the poodles illustrated in Colour Plates 99 and 110.

The bitch and three puppies group of Colour Plate 88 and the bitch modelled independently and illustrated in Colour Plate 89 are, of course, from the same factory. The former is inscribed under the base in red script '37', the latter '38'. The bitch of Colour Plate 88 is unclipped, but this is not always the case.[76]

A careful comparison of the group of Colour Plate 88 with the pointer and three puppies shown in Colour Plate 195 (inscribed under the base '112' in red) will reveal

COLOUR PLATE 82. *Pair of Staffordshire poodles, each lying recumbent on a pink cushion base. 3in. long. c.1840–50.*

COLOUR PLATE 83. *Staffordshire group consisting of a poodle bitch and two puppies on a cushion base covered with drapes decorated in pink. 3¼in. long. c.1840–50.*

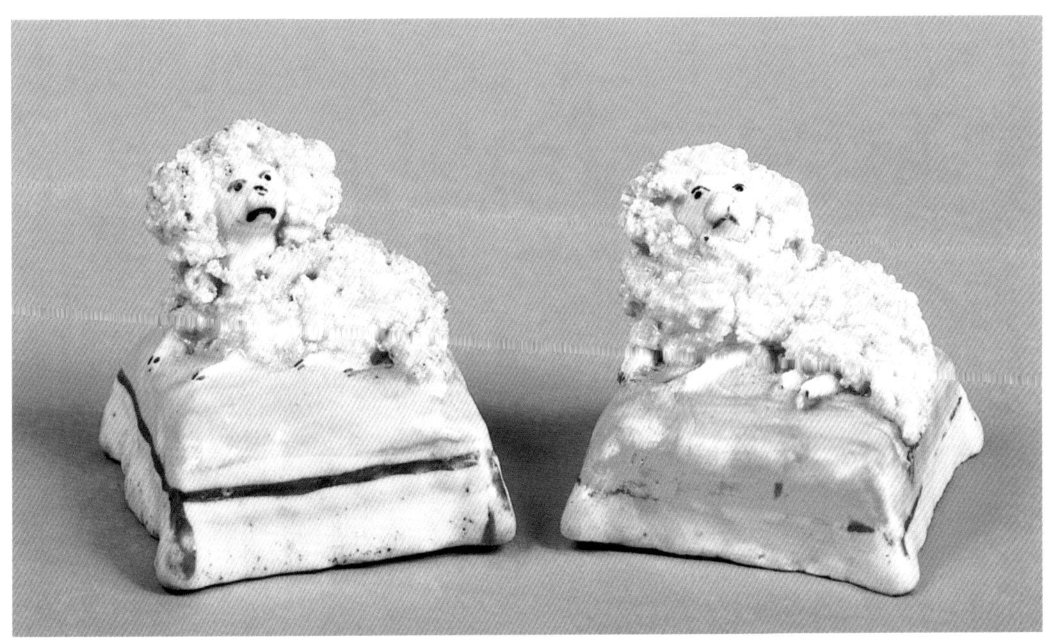

COLOUR PLATE 84. *Two Staffordshire toy poodles each lying recumbent on a square pink cushion with tassels. 1½in. wide. c.1840–50.*

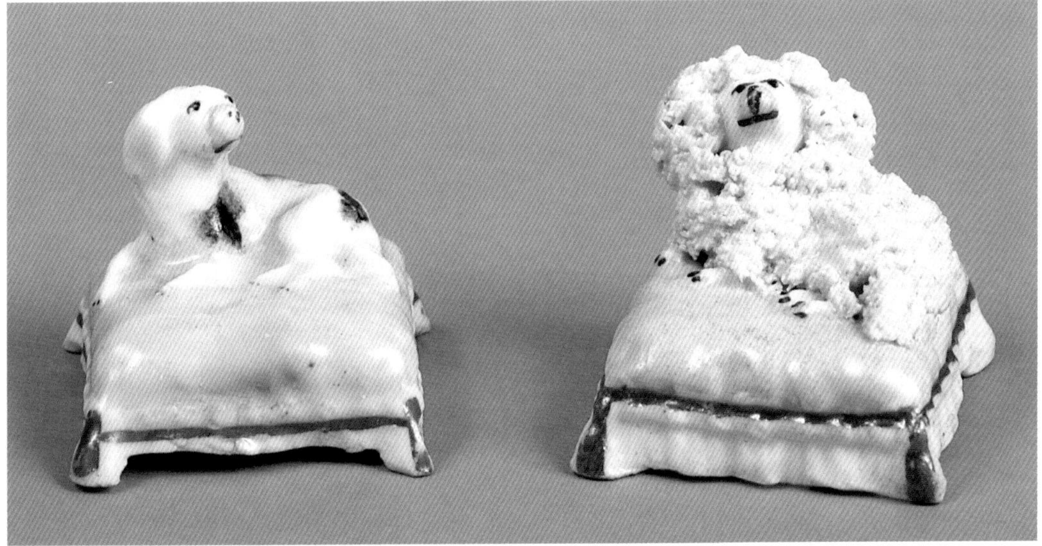

COLOUR PLATE 85.
a. (left). Staffordshire toy King Charles spaniel lying recumbent on a yellow cushion base supported on four tasselled legs. 1½in. wide. c.1830–50.
b. (right). Staffordshire toy poodle lying recumbent on a square yellow cushion base with tassels. 1⅝in. wide. c.1840–50.

that the bitch is essentially the same in both cases. The pose and size are identical and the puppies, although one of them is placed in a different position to accommodate a different base, are likewise essentially the same. The only difference lies in the details of modelling necessary to represent, in the one case a poodle and puppies with their distinctive wool, and in the other a pointer and puppies with their smooth coats. Clearly the same factory was responsible for both groups.[77]

The bitch executed as an independent model has as its companion a poodle dog with an arched back seated on the same type base.[78] Having regard to the positioning of their bodies, these two animals are essentially reversed, but strangely because the bitch looks backwards and the dog straight ahead, they effectively look in the same direction. But that they are a true pair is clear from a comparison with the pair of foxhounds shown

COLOUR PLATE 86. *Pair of Staffordshire poodles, each seated on a flat cushion base, in one case green, in the other purple. 3in. high. c.1835–50. This model is also recorded on a simple white and gilt base.*

COLOUR PLATE 87. *Staffordshire poodle seated on a gilt-banded base with concave corners. 3½in. high. c.1830–50.*

COLOUR PLATE 88. *Staffordshire unclipped poodle bitch with three puppies on an elaborately scrolled base with gilt embellishments. 5in. high. Inscribed under the base with the number '37' in red. Possibly Dudson. c.1830–50.*

COLOUR PLATE 89. *The poodle of the group of Colour Plate 88 (but with the lion-clip) as an independent model. 5in. high. Inscribed under the base with the number '38' in red. Possibly Dudson. c.1830–50.*

in Colour Plate 203. The one that looks back corresponds to the poodle bitch, whilst the hound with arched back that looks straight ahead corresponds to the poodle dog. Seemingly the hounds and poodles were made by the same factory. That the hounds are themselves a true pair is demonstrated by the fact that the same models appear together again elsewhere[79] and were also produced in pottery as companions to each other. Manifestly, if the hounds are a pair, so too must be the poodles.[80]

The poodle of Colour Plate 87 has a particularly endearing face. In contrast, the expression of the poodle of Colour Plate 90 is lion-like and quite ferocious, clearly not a dog to be trifled with. The thick gilt band running continuously around the edge of the base is the only decoration; there are not even any facial markings. The same model appears in biscuit (Colour Plate 91). Although unidentified, the model is clearly the product of an important Staffordshire factory. Otherwise, the high quality wool, made of threads of porcelain, could not have been produced.

Staffordshire poodles in a standing position with a basket of coloured flowers in the mouth are reasonably common (see, for example, Colour Plates 100–102). But not so Staffordshire poodles standing on a base with painted flowers, examples of which can

Colour Plate 90. *Staffordshire poodle with lion-like face, but no facial markings, lying on a two-tiered rectangular platform edged with a continuous thick gilt band. 3½in. long. c.1830–50.*

Colour Plate 91. *The biscuit version of the poodle of Colour Plate 90. Where the animal is unclipped, the wool is represented by individual threads of porcelain.*

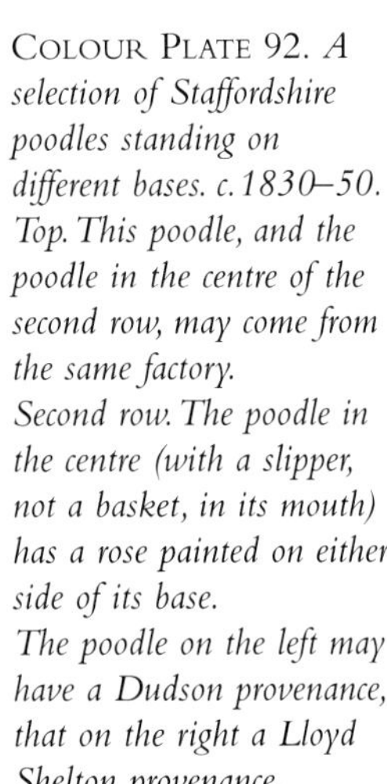

Colour Plate 92. *A selection of Staffordshire poodles standing on different bases. c.1830–50. Top. This poodle, and the poodle in the centre of the second row, may come from the same factory. Second row. The poodle in the centre (with a slipper, not a basket, in its mouth) has a rose painted on either side of its base. The poodle on the left may have a Dudson provenance, that on the right a Lloyd Shelton provenance.*
Christie's South Kensington

COLOUR PLATE 93. *Staffordshire poodle with a black hat in its mouth, standing on a rectangular mound base with slanting edges painted with roses and leaves. 3in. high. c.1835–50.*

COLOUR PLATE 94. *Staffordshire poodle, unclipped, except for the front legs, lying recumbent on a lilac shaped rectangular base, moulded with elaborate scrolling. 5in. long. c.1835–50. The lilac colour of the base is not applied simply to the surface of the porcelain but permeates it through and through.*

Andrew Dando Antiques

COLOUR PLATE 95. *Staffordshire poodle with 'lion clip' lying recumbent on a lilac shaped rectangular base moulded with elaborate scrolling. 5in. long. c.1835–50. As in the case of Colour Plate 94, the lilac colour of the base permeates the porcelain.*

Andrew Dando Antiques

COLOUR PLATE 96.
Staffordshire parti-coloured poodle lying recumbent with hindquarters raised, on a burnt-orange shaped rectangular base moulded with scrolls. 3½in. long. c.1835–50. Compare the poodle of Colour Plate 19b. This model comes from the factory responsible for the animals appearing in Colour Plates 18 and 147.

COLOUR PLATE 97.
Staffordshire black and white poodle seated on a rectangular cushion base with tassels, edged with a continuous gilt line. 3⅛in. high. c.1840–50. Compare Colour Plate 114.

COLOUR PLATE 98.
Staffordshire black poodle, standing on a rectangular stool supported by angled paw feet. 3in. high. c.1830–50.

COLOUR PLATE 99. *Staffordshire group of two poodles, one seated, the other lying down, on a shaped base, cobalt-blue and cream. 2½in. long. c.1840–50.*

COLOUR PLATE 100. *Staffordshire white and gilt poodle, with a basket of flowers in its mouth, standing on an extremely rocky mound base. 2in. long. c.1840–50.*

COLOUR PLATE 101. *Staffordshire poodle, with an orange basket in its mouth, standing on a scrolled mound base. 3¼in. high. c.1840–50.*

COLOUR PLATE 102. *Staffordshire poodle, with an orange basket in its mouth, standing on a scrolled mound base. 2⅞in. high. c.1840–50.*

COLOUR PLATE 103. *Staffordshire poodle, with an orange basket in its mouth, standing on a lightly scrolled mound base encrusted most unusually with sea-shells. 3½in. high. c.1840–50.*

be seen in Colour Plates 93, 104 and 105. (That of Colour Plate 93 is particularly interesting because the dog holds in its mouth a black hat.) Occasionally, Staffordshire poodles were modelled begging (Colour Plate 81, centre). Sometimes a poodle is accompanied by a human figure (Colour Plate 75 – the two groups are not identical but vary slightly,[81] and Colour Plate 108). But usually poodles were produced as independent models.

Interestingly, the Staffordshire factories often turned out miniatures or toys.[82] A selection is shown here (e.g. Colour Plates 81, 84, 85, 112, 113 and 120). The poodles standing on a deep rectangular base shown in Colour Plate 115 are somewhat crude in modelling. But interestingly, the wool is of the pebble-dash variety (i.e. not formed of encrusted granules or porcelain threads) corresponding to the thinly applied wool on the puppies of Colour Plate 88. The thought suggests itself that there might be a common manufacturer, one which though capable of high quality work, might want to reach a wider market where price was all important and might in furtherance of this objective issue a cheap run of poodles. By the late 1840s the population was growing fast, and with industrial development those in employment had more money than ever before. But they could afford little on luxuries, so that manufacturers who wanted to tap this vast expanding market had to sell at an attractive price.

The various poodles represented here are sufficiently described in the captions to require no further comment beyond that already made.

COLOUR PLATE 104. *Staffordshire poodle standing on a flower-decorated base (with pink roses and green leaves in the front and wild flowers at the rear) supported by ball feet, and holding in its mouth a pale-mauve game bird. 4in. high. c.1835–50.*

COLOUR PLATE 105. *Staffordshire poodle, with a basket of flowers in its mouth, standing on a mound base with sloping slightly concave sides, painted on the front with a rose and forget-me-nots, and on both ends with forget-me-nots alone. 3⅞in. high. c.1835–50.*

COLOUR PLATE 106. *Pair of Staffordshire poodles, each holding a white and gilt game bird in its mouth, and standing on a rectangular tiered plinth in turn resting on four paw feet. 3⅝in. high. c.1835–50.*

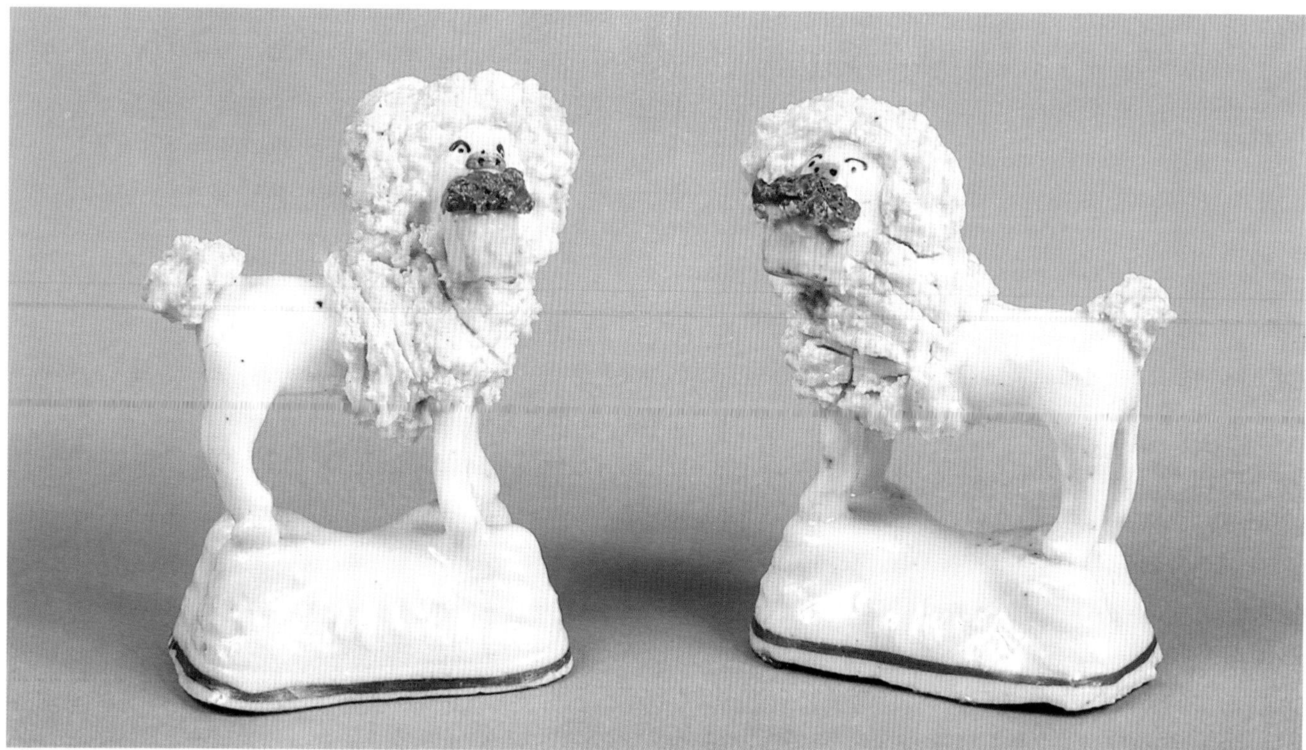

Colour Plate 107. *Pair of Staffordshire poodles, each holding in its mouth a yellow basket filled with greenery, and standing on a mound base (with pinched-in sides) edged with a continuous gilt line. 2½in. high. c.1835–50.*

Colour Plate 108. *Staffordshire seated girl with a pink dress feeding her poodle out of a deep bowl, on a shaped base. 3¾in. high. c.1840–50.*

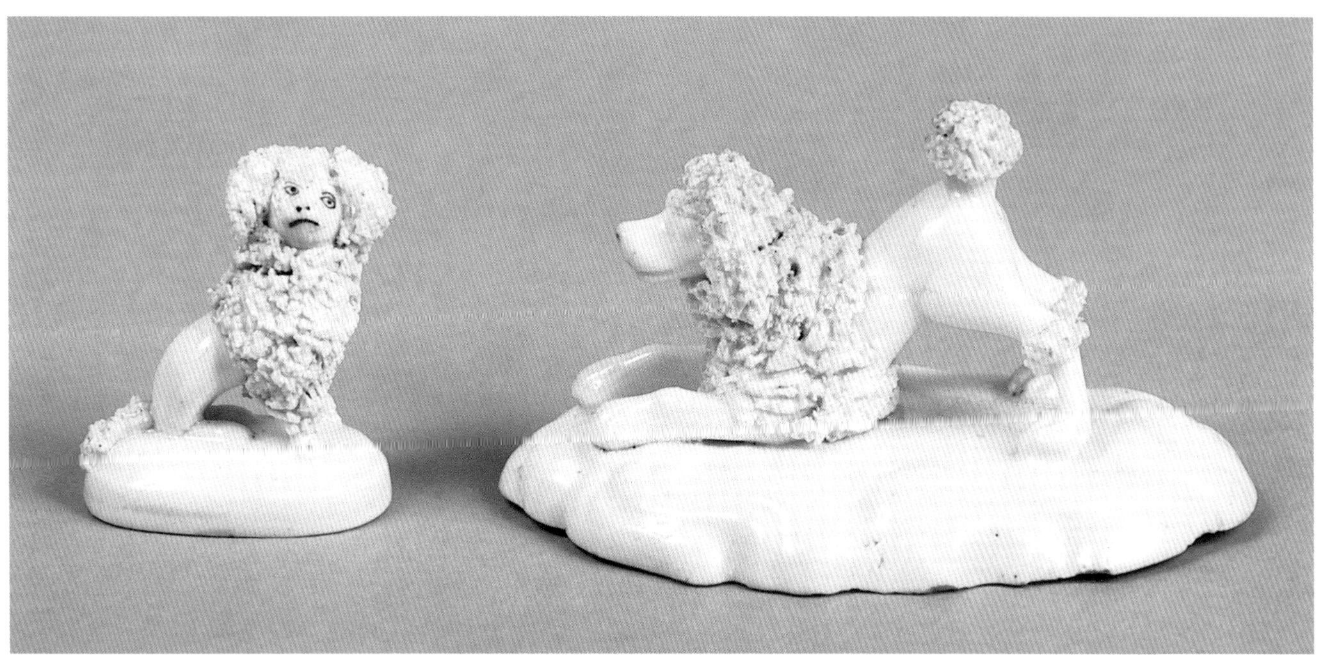

COLOUR PLATE 109. *a. (left). Staffordshire toy poodle seated on an oval mound base. 1½in. high. c.1830–50. b. (right). Staffordshire white-glazed poodle with upraised hind legs lying recumbent on a shaped moulded base. 3⅜in. long. c.1835–50. Note the distinctive moulding of the base indicating a common origin with the King Charles spaniel of Colour Plates 145 and 146. Sometimes this model has its front paw about to descend on a naturally coloured rat.*

COLOUR PLATE 110. *Staffordshire poodle lying on a cobalt-blue mound base. 2⅛in. long. c.1840–50.*

COLOUR PLATE 111. *Staffordshire poodle with coloured wool seated on a distinctive scrolled base embellished with gilding. 3½in. high. c.1835–50. This model was made in reverse to form a pair.*

Andrew Dando Antiques

COLOUR PLATE 112. *a. (left). Staffordshire poodle with black hat in its mouth standing on a rectangular mound base with sloping sides. 2in. high. c.1835–50.*
b. (right). Staffordshire toy poodle seated on a rectangular base with sloping sides edged with a continuous gilt line. 1⅝in. high. c.1835–50.

COLOUR PLATE 113. *Pair of Staffordshire toy poodles, each seated on a mound base with concave edges. 2in. high. Mark: ·√ in black. c.1835–50.*

COLOUR PLATE 114. *Staffordshire black and white poodle seated on a royal-blue rectangular cushion base with white tassels, edged with a continuous gilt line. 3⅛in. high. c.1840–50. Compare Colour Plate 97.*

COLOUR PLATE 115. *Pair of Staffordshire poodles, each standing on a deep rectangular base with rounded corners, together with a single example, in the centre, from the same factory on a base edged with a gilt line. 2⅜in. high. c.1840–50.*

COLOUR PLATE 116. *Staffordshire poodle and cat group, the poodle stopping short outside its moss-encrusted kennel at the sight of a tortoiseshell cat poised with outstretched tail. 5in. long. c.1835–50.*

COLOUR PLATE 117.
Staffordshire poodle and cat group, the cat emerging aggressively from a kennel decorated in beige, whilst the poodle stands its ground, on a deep rocky base with a gilt line. c.1835–50.

COLOUR PLATE 118.
Staffordshire poodle and cat group, the poodle half out of its turf- and moss-covered kennel, looking at a somewhat playful cat, on a mound base. 3⅝in. long. c.1835–50.

Oliver-Sutton Antiques

COLOUR PLATE 119. *Staffordshire toy poodle lying outside its kennel decorated in apricot with a pink roof, on a rectangular base with rounded corners. 3in. long. c.1840–50.*

COLOUR PLATE 120. *Staffordshire toy poodle standing outside its kennel on a flower-encrusted base in lavender. 3½in. long; together with a larger example. 4⅛in. long. c.1835–50. The lavender colour of the bases is not simply applied to the surface of the porcelain, but permeates it.*

COLOUR PLATE 121. *Staffordshire poodle, scrutinising a duck, on a cobalt-blue base edged with a continuous gilt line. 2½in. long. c.1840–50*

Samson Reproductions

It is not without interest to note that Samson of Paris, the well-known reproducer in *hard* paste of the products of all the leading English factories, also fabricated during the last part of the nineteenth century (and the early part of the twentieth century) imitations of typical poodles of the period 1830–50. A pair appeared at the Ardingly Antiques Fair of April 1994. They each had about the head, knee joints and tail the typical fuzzy wool associated with poodles (represented by means of porcelain threads) and stood on deep blue rectangular bases with rounded corners, supported in turn on four bun feet. Each held in its mouth a light-blue basket, and under the base Samson of Paris had fraudulently painted the Chelsea gold anchor mark.

COLOUR PLATE 122. *Rockingham white and gilt springer spaniel running on a rocky gilt-splashed base. 3¼in. long. Incised 'No 83'. Cl. 1. Impressed mark. 1826–30.*

COLOUR PLATE 123. *Rockingham plaque depicting a spaniel chasing game; signed on the reverse by 'Bailey'. Length 5½in., height 4¼in. Red Griffin mark. The dog of Colour Plate 122 seems to be a three-dimensional representation of this.*

COLOUR PLATE 124. *White and brown springer spaniel running, on a hollow base splashed with green and gold. 4¼in. long. This is a copy of Rockingham No 83, made by Samson of Paris. c.1870, and fraudulently marked with a Chelsea gold anchor (see p.81).*

SPANIELS

SPORTING SPANIELS

During the nineteenth century the spaniel was a particular favourite of sportsmen, having an origin going back to the fourteenth century. There were different varieties – springer spaniels, cocker spaniels and water spaniels, each with its own special qualities. Engravings of springer spaniels are to be found in, among other places, Daniel's *Rural Sports*, Taplin's *Sportsman's Cabinet* and J.G. Wood's *The Illustrated Natural History*. Taplin observes of this breed:

> It was delicately formed with ears long, soft and pliable, coat waving and silky, eyes and nose red or black, the tail somewhat bulky and pendulous, always in motion when actively employed.

Springer spaniels derived their name from their inherent ability 'to spring, flush or start all the game before them, and they pursue, without preference, hare, pheasant, partridge, woodcock, snipe and quail'. The Cocker spaniel (illustrated in Wood) was in contrast smaller than the springer. It found the scent more easily and, being shorter and more compact,

COLOUR PLATE 125. *King Street Derby springer spaniel in biscuit lying recumbent on a rectangular base. 3⅞in. long. Later nineteenth century.*

COLOUR PLATE 126.
a. (left). Rockingham setter with black patches lying recumbent on a rectangular base in white and green edged with a gilt line, 4¼in. long. Incised 'No 94'. Cl. 2. 1826–30. For other examples of this model see Colour Plates 165 and 166 and Figure 9b.
b. (right). Rockingham cocker spaniel with brown patches, lying curled up on a rectangular base. 2⅝in. long. Incised 'No 91' 1826–30. For a biscuit example see Figure 9a.

COLOUR PLATE 127. *Derby cocker spaniel with brown patches lying curled up on a black rectangular base. 3⅛in. long. c.1820–45. Compare the Rockingham version in reverse, Colour Plate 126b and Figure 9a.*

could push its way through low bushy cover. It was chiefly employed in woodcock shooting – hence its name 'cocker spaniel'. Water spaniels accompanied wildfowlers, and an engraving of one of them appears in Taplin's frontispiece. The breed is now extinct.

Rockingham

The spaniel as a sporting dog is to be found among the animals turned out at Swinton. The white and gilt model (No 83) illustrated in Colour Plate 122 would seem to be a springer spaniel and was clearly intended to be a three-dimensional version of the dog in the Rockingham plaque illustrated in Colour Plate 123.[83]

The enamelled and gilt springer of Colour Plate 124 looks remarkably like the Rockingham white and gold dog of Colour Plate 122. It is decorated with brown patches, and stands on a rocky white and green base splashed, in a typical Rockingham way, with gilding. However, it is in fact a copy, being probably the work of Samson of Paris, who from 1870 onwards reproduced everything that was then collectable in porcelain. It is made of *hard* paste and the underside of the base is not constructed in the Rockingham fashion, i.e. made flat and closed-in save for a centrally located hole, but instead is deeply recessed. Also, notwithstanding that the piece has no similarity whatsoever with anything the Chelsea factory produced, it carries the Chelsea gold anchor mark on the top of the base, adjacent to the dog's right back leg.

Looking at the animal in isolation, it is difficult to say whether the dog of Colour Plate 126b and Figure 9a is a cocker spaniel or a setter. The factory applied no consistency of scale (the terriers of Colour Plate 218 and 219 are almost as big as the mastiff of Colour Plate 197), and there is simply nothing by which to make a dimensional comparison. However, I consider that it is more likely to be a spaniel, probably a cocker spaniel, than a setter, and accordingly I classify as such.

A companion model has been discovered (Colour Plate 127). It is somewhat larger than the animals of Colour Plate 126b and Figure 9a. This is not necessary fatal to a Rockingham attribution, the factory frequently making models in more than one size, but it is not possible with any confidence to ascribe a Rockingham provenance.

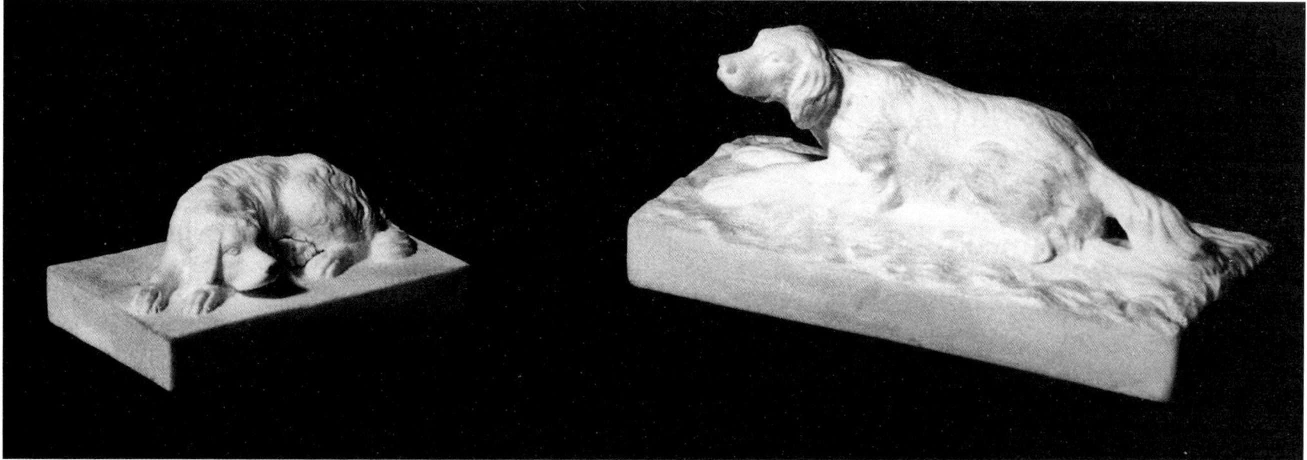

FIGURE 9. a. *(left). Rockingham cocker spaniel in biscuit, curled up on a rectangular base. 2⅝in. long. Incised 'No 91'. Impressed mark. 1826–30. For a coloured example see Colour Plate 126b.*
b. (right). Rockingham setter in biscuit, lying recumbent on a rectangular base. 4¼in. long. Incised 'No 94'. Impressed mark. 1826–30. For a coloured example see Colour Plates 126a, 165 and 166.

Derby Factory (Nottingham Road)
The spaniel of Colour Plate 127, if it does not originate from the Rockingham factory, must necessarily have come from Derby. There is some evidence to suggest that this model is linked with William Coffee, in that a version in a kind of unglazed creamware is recorded signed on the upper side of the base 'W. Coffee'.[84]

Derby Factory (King Street)
The biscuit animal shown in Colour Plate 125 is probably from the King Street factory, Derby. The underneath of the base is closed in save for a centrally located hole. The biscuit is of the type found at the King Street factory, not the true white and chalky variety which features at the Nottingham Road factory, but instead ivory in colour with a slight glaze to the surface, somewhat akin to Parian. King Street biscuit animals are rare.[85] Normally, the animals are glazed-white or coloured.

Chamberlain Worcester
That the Chamberlain factory did turn out spaniels is established by the reference contained in certain factory documents of January 1823[86]:

3 small Spaniel dogs 2s 0d

As no porcelain example has been recorded so far, it is impossible to say what Chamberlain Worcester spaniels actually looked like, and in particular whether they were in the form of sporting dogs or King Charles spaniels.

Grainger Lee & Co., Worcester
A spaniel appears in the factory's pattern book, but this would appear to represent, not a sporting dog, but a King Charles spaniel.

Minton and Other Factories
No example has so far been recorded of a sporting, as distinct from a King Charles, spaniel.

KING CHARLES SPANIELS
Toy spaniels were known on the continent from the fifteenth century onwards. They appear regularly on canvases, from Titian's painting of the Duchess of Urbino,[87] executed in 1538, onwards and before that on tapestries (see the Arras tapestry 'The Offering of the Heart'). In a painting by Antonio Moro, executed in 1554,[88] a pair of spaniels are represented at the feet of Mary I and her husband Philip of Spain. In 1563 a small dog accompanied Mary Queen of Scots at her execution, and this is thought to have been a toy spaniel. A year earlier Steven Van der Meulin painted a portrait of a woman, probably Catherine Carey, Lady Knollys.[89] A toy spaniel is depicted standing prominently on a table in front of her. However, this breed of lap-dog is particularly associated with King Charles I, and even more so with his son Charles II. Hence the name 'King Charles' spaniel.

These dogs appear regularly in the works of Van Dyck, Watteau, Boucher and Greuze, invariably as a small animal with a flat head, long nose, soft fleecy coat, and curly tail, and always hyperactive. They were brown/white, black/white, or tricolour. In 1678 Peter Lely painted Lady Temple 'with her favourite spaniel' (she was an enthusiastic owner of many spaniels). He also executed a portrait of Miss Skipwith with an almost life-size toy spaniel.

Pepys in his diary refers to these dogs when on an occasion in September 1666 he visited the Council Chamber: 'All I observed was the silliness of the King playing with his dogs all the while and not minding the business'. In 1867, 'Stonehenge' made an interesting reference to the association of King Charles II with his small dogs:

> The old President of Magdalen College, who died about 10 years ago in his hundredth year, was accustomed to say that when he was a little boy he had been told by an old lady that when she was a little girl she saw the King round the Magdalen walks with these little dogs.

The attachment of the King to his dogs is vividly illustrated by an advertisement which he caused to appear in the *Mercurius Publicus* as the result of the loss of what was a crossbreed between a spaniel and an Italian greyhound:

> We must call upon you for a black dog, in breed betwixt a greyhound and a spaniel, no white about him, only a streak on his breast, and his tail a little bobbed. It is his Majesty's own dog and doubtless was stolen, for the dog was not born or bred in England and would never forsake his master. Will they never leave robbing his Majesty? Must he not keep a dog? The dog's place is the only one about the Court that nobody begs for.

One wonders, in view of the obvious feeling contained in the advertisement whether his Majesty was personally responsible for its terms.

John Evelyn positively disliked King Charles spaniels. In a posthumous assessment of the King he wrote:

> He took delight in having a number of little spaniels to follow him and lie in his bedchamber and where he often suffered his bitches to puppy and give suck which rendered it offensive, and indeed made the whole Court nasty and stinking.

James II also adored these toy spaniels, but on the fall of the Stuarts, the dogs went out of fashion and were replaced in popularity by the pug.

However, the King Charles spaniel did not disappear altogether, and from the beginning of William IV's reign it seems to have enjoyed something of a revival. Later, during Victoria's reign, the breed underwent certain changes: the long nose shortened and the flat head became domed. Doubtless a cross was introduced, probably by means of a pug dog. The modified breed continues today. In the late Victorian period, the original version became virtually extinct, but in 1928 breeders decided to recreate it, and this is called the 'Cavalier'. All the porcelain replicas of the non-sporting spaniel illustrated here are of the dog in its original form.

It is perhaps worth remarking that King Charles spaniels in porcelain would seem not to have been produced in the nineteenth century before about 1830, or, if they were, not to any significant extent. There are a few examples belonging to the eighteenth century but thereafter the dog itself would appear to have fallen out of favour for a period, and this was reflected in the absence, or virtual absence, of china representations. From around 1830 onwards, however, the King Charles was turned out by such major factories as Minton, Grainger Lee, Copeland & Garrett and Samuel Alcock, and to an ever-increasing extent up to about 1850, by the numerous unidentified factories operating in Staffordshire.

Rockingham
No Rockingham King Charles spaniel as an independent model has so far been recorded. However, the dog which is leaping up on to the boy of model No 35 (Figure 10) would seem to be a King Charles. This particular group would appear to have been modelled by George Cocker, and is more frequently found in Derby porcelain.

Derby (Nottingham Road)
Apart from the dog appearing in the Derby version of the Rockingham model No 35 referred to above, the only nineteenth century King Charles spaniel attributable to the Derby factory at Nottingham Road so far identified is the one that accompanies the girl of model No 71.

Derby (King Street)
However, a Sampson Hancock pair of King Charles spaniels is recorded. Such a pair in biscuit, lying recumbent 3¾in. long, carried the Sampson Hancock mark in blue.[90]

Grainger Lee & Co., Worcester
A spaniel appears in the factory's pattern book. However, so far no porcelain example is recorded.

Royal Worcester
In 1874 the Royal Worcester factory turned out two separate models of a King Charles spaniel (items 387 and 410 respectively in the factory list). However, it is not clear whether they were ever made in porcelain.

FIGURE 10. *Rockingham King Charles spaniel leaping up on to a boy standing on a circular pierced scroll base, in biscuit. 5¾in. high. Incised 'No 35'. Impressed mark. 1826–30.*

FIGURE 11. *Minton King Charles spaniel in Parian lying recumbent on a cushion base with tassels. 4in. long. Model No 22. Incised 'July 19 1849'. For a coloured example see Colour Plate 128.*
Godden of Worthing Ltd.

COLOUR PLATE 128. *Minton black and white King Charles spaniel lying recumbent on a puce cushion base with yellow tassels. Model No 22. 4in. long. c.1831–40. For an example in Parian see Figure 11.*

Minton

The Minton King Charles illustrated in Colour Plate 128 is model No 22 in the factory drawing book. The same model also appears in biscuit, and in white and gold. It was also turned out in Parian (Figure 11).

Further, the same model was made to lie on a long narrow rectangular mound base encrusted with flowers and berries to form a paperweight (Figure 12).

The only other spaniel model known as coming from the Minton factory is a King Charles standing on a tasselled cushion in a begging pose. It is numbered 32 in the

FIGURE 12. *Minton King Charles spaniel with brown patches, lying recumbent on a narrow rounded rectangular base encrusted with flowers and berries. 8½in. long. Interlaced Ls mark in blue. c.1831–40.*
Sotheby's

COLOUR PLATE 129. *Minton spill-holder group in biscuit: a King Charles spaniel, standing on its hind legs, is begging food from a young girl, whilst a cat is feeding from a plate at the feet of a sleeping child. 5in. high. c.1831–45.*

drawing book. No example in porcelain is recorded as an independent model, but it appears as part of a spill-holder illustrated in Colour Plate 129 (presumably after an unidentified print). A small girl seated on an upturned basket, is encouraging the dog to beg for food kept in a pot on her lap, whilst a younger sister has fallen asleep besides a hollow tree trunk, leaving a cat to help itself to milk/food in a bowl at her feet. That the group comes from the Minton factory is clear from the presence of the dog model No 32. Moreover, the dress and general appearance of the girl feeding the dog is very similar to 'Good Night' (Model No 11). Further, the base is moulded in the same rococo style typical of the Minton factory at that time. A puzzling feature of the group, however, is that it is not referred to in the factory drawing book. However, several of the factory's models are neither described nor illustrated in the book. It is interesting to note that model No 49 comprises a boy playing with a dog, whilst model No 50 has no title or illustration. Perhaps the group of Colour Plate 129 is to be identified with Model No 50.

COLOUR PLATE 130. *Copeland & Garrett brown and white King Charles spaniel lying recumbent on an elaborately scrolled base picked out in gold. 4½in.long. Factory mark. 1833–47.*

Copeland & Garrett

The Copeland & Garrett factory produced the King Charles spaniel illustrated in Colour Plate 130. It also turned out a much larger model. An example appeared at the London Ceramics Fair in June 1993. The animal, with black patches, lay recumbent on a crimson rectangular base with rounded corners, some 8in. long. Under the base there was to be seen the factory's printed mark. Another example, but this time on a blue cushion base with gilt tassels, was exhibited at the London Ceramics Fair in January 1996. Other examples appear on a green base. A variant of this model was shown at the Grosvenor House Art and Antiques Fair of 1996, where a black and white bitch recumbent on a crimson cushion base (printed underneath with the factory mark) was accompanied by three puppies.

Davenport

Whether or not the great Davenport factory produced any porcelain animals is not certain (see pp.167), but if it did, this would seem to be the most likely provenance of the King Charles spaniel bitch shown in Colour Plate 131. The modelling is fine, the gold band around the base rich, and the piece generally heavy in weight. The glazing is affected by crazing. Doubtless there was originally a companion *dog* in reverse.

COLOUR PLATE 131. *White and brown King Charles spaniel lying recumbent on a green mound supported in turn by a black rectangular base edged with a thick gold band. 2⁷⁄₁₆in. long. Probably from the Davenport factory. c.1830–50*

COLOUR PLATE 132. *On the right, Samuel Alcock King Charles spaniel with brown patches seated on a yellow mound base. 5in. high. Impressed '121'; together with the free-standing version, left. 4in. high. c.1840–50. Note the minor variations of the latter to allow for the omission of the base.*

Samuel Alcock

Various versions of King Charles spaniels are recorded as made by Samuel Alcock. Models numbered 18 or 81 (Colour Plates 136 and 137), 25 (Colour Plate 134a), 121 (Colour Plate 132), 125 (Colour Plate 133a), and 183 (Colour Plate 133b) are here illustrated. In addition, there are two further models. One (Colour Plate 134b) is impressed underneath with the numeral '2', but this number would appear to be only part of a higher number not properly impressed. The other model, the number of which

COLOUR PLATE 133. *a. (left). Samuel Alcock King Charles spaniel with brown patches seated on a yellow mound base with a gilt line. 3in. high. Impressed '125', possibly an error for '183'. c.1840–50. b. (right). The same model but impressed '183'. For a pair see Figure 13.*

COLOUR PLATE 134.
a. (left). Samuel Alcock King Charles spaniel with black patches lying recumbent on a yellow rectangular mound base with rounded corners and edged with a gilt line. 2¼in. long. Impressed '25' c.1835–50.
b. (right) Samuel Alcock King Charles spaniel with black patches seated upright on a heavily scrolled mound base in yellow 2¼in. high. Impressed '2', seemingly an incomplete number. c.1835–50.

is not recorded, is shown in Colour Plate 135. The dog appears to be a King Charles spaniel and sits upright on an octagonal base moulded with leaves.

An example of model No 25 was, together with other animals produced by the factory, buried in April 1839 under the foundation stone of the new factory building, but only the base impressed '25' survives. The illustration in Colour Plate 134a reveals what the animal looked like.

It is difficult to see any difference between Nos 125 and 183, and it may be that '125' is a mistake for '183' made by the factory. I suggest that '125', rather than '183', is the wrong number because, although no other example of the model has been found

FIGURE 13. *Pair of Samuel Alcock King Charles spaniels with brown and black markings, each seated upright on a yellow mound base. 3⅛in. high. Impressed '183'. c.1840–50. For another example see Colour Plate 133b.*
Christie's South Kensington

impressed '125', three examples are recorded impressed '183'. One is illustrated in Colour Plate 133b, whilst the other two – in fact a pair – are shown in Figure 13.

Not illustrated here is the Samuel Alcock model No 222. It consists of a seated King Charles bitch with two puppies, the latter standing on their hind legs playing with the bitch. The group is 4¼in. high overall, and the base is moulded to take a small inkwell. Likewise not illustrated is a begging King Charles spaniel with a black hat (No. 329).

Finally, reference should be made to the King Charles spaniel seated upright which accompanies the pug in the group impressed '342' (Colour Plate 36).

Colour Plate 135. *Samuel Alcock King Charles toy spaniel with brown markings seated on a yellow octagonal base moulded with leaves. 1¾in. high. c.1835–50.* Phillips

Colour Plate 136. *Two Samuel Alcock King Charles spaniels, black and white, each lying on a yellow scrolled mound base. 3in. long. Impressed '18' or '81'. c.1835–50.*

Colour Plate 137. *Two Samuel Alcock King Charles spaniels, one brown and white lying on a green scroll mound base, the other black and white, lying on a yellow scrolled mound base. Impressed '18' or '81'. 3in. long. c.1835–50. These are the reverse of the models of Colour Plate 136.*

FIGURE 14. *Madeley King Charles spaniel lying recumbent on a bright-blue rectangular cushion base with gilt tassels. 3½in. long. c.1830.* Christie's

Madeley

One of the very rare animals to have survived from the Madeley factory is the King Charles spaniel shown in Figure 14. It is made of the factory's peculiar hard type paste.[91]

Dudson

Illustrated in Figure 15 is a group of three spaniels from the Dudson factory found on the factory site. The group shown is earthenware, but the model might have been produced in porcelain as well.[92]

FIGURE 15. *Dudson group of three red spaniels seated on a blue quill-holder base. 5in. long. c.1845. This group excavated at the factory site is in pottery, although the same model may have been made in porcelain.* Mrs. Audrey Dudson

COLOUR PLATE 138. *a. (left). Staffordshire Newfoundland, being ridden by a small boy in a green jacket, standing on a white and gilt rectangular mound base with rounded corners. 3¼in. long. c.1835–50.*
b. (right). Staffordshire King Charles spaniel, decorated with iron red patches, recumbent on a mound base applied with foliage. 4in. long. c.1835–50. Christie's South Kensington

COLOUR PLATE 139. *Staffordshire King Charles spaniel and puppy, with liver markings, the former seated upright, the latter lying recumbent, on a rectangular mound base with rounded corners and moulded scrolls, edged with a black (not gilt) line. 3in. long. c.1835–50.*

COLOUR PLATE 140. *Staffordshire King Charles spaniel and puppy decorated in black and ochre, the puppy turned away from the bitch, on a green rectangular base with rounded corners. 2⅞in. high. c.1835–50. The reverse model appears to be a cat and kitten.* Christie's South Kensington

Unidentified Staffordshire Factories

King Charles spaniels were, during the period 1830–50, turned out by various unidentified Staffordshire factories on a prolific scale, almost as prolific as were the contemporary poodles. A selection of such spaniels are illustrated here.

COLOUR PLATE 141. *Staffordshire begging King Charles spaniel, its coat painted with patches of brown, on a green mound base, painted '217' underneath. 3in. high. 1835–50.* Christie's South Kensington

COLOUR PLATE 142. *Staffordshire King Charles Spaniel with brown markings confronting a black and white tabby cat taking refuge on a low tree-trunk, on a tiered white base. 3⅞in. high. c.1840–50.* Phillips

COLOUR PLATE 143.
Staffordshire King Charles spaniel with black patches lying recumbent on a green cushion base with gilt and white tassels. 3⅜in. long. c.1835–50.

COLOUR PLATE 144.
Staffordshire King Charles spaniel with black patches lying recumbent on a green cushion base with gilt tassels. 2⅜in. long. c.1835–50.

COLOUR PLATE 145.
Staffordshire King Charles spaniel, black and white lying recumbent on a shaped oval scrolled base encrusted with coloured flowers. 3⅜in. long. c.1835–50. Compare this with the unencrusted version in Colour Plate 146.

COLOUR PLATE 146. *a. (left). Staffordshire King Charles spaniel with brown patches lying recumbent on a shaped oval base with scrolled mouldings edged with a continuous gilt line. 3⅞in. long. Inscribed under the base in black '134'. c.1835–50.*
b. (right). The reverse model, with black patches lying recumbent on a similarly shaped base splashed with gold. 3⅞in. long. This model also appears on a dark blue base with white and gilt edges. The factory responsible for this model also produced the poodle of Colour Plate 109b.

COLOUR PLATE 147. *Staffordshire white and brown spaniel lying recumbent on a rare turquoise shaped scrolled base. 3½in. long. c.1835–50. The more decorative scrolling of the base is at the rear. The factory responsible for this model also produced the greyhounds of Colour Plate 18 and the poodle of Colour Plate 96.*

COLOUR PLATE 148. *Pair of Staffordshire King Charles spaniels with liver markings, each seated on a shaped rectangular white and puce base. 2⅝in. high. c.1840–50.*

COLOUR PLATE 149. *Staffordshire King Charles spaniel with black feathered patches seated on a rectangular base with canted corners. 3⅛in. high. Impressed under the base with a faint '1', possibly part of a 'T' indicating a particular factory production batch. c.1840–50.*

COLOUR PLATE 150. *Staffordshire King Charles spaniel stopping short, with a small support, head turned, tail raised, on a rectangular cushion base with pink edges and gilt tassels. 2¾in. long. Inscribed under the base '204' in red. c.1835–50.*

COLOUR PLATE 151. *a. (left). Staffordshire King Charles spaniel with black patches and elaborate fluffy tail seated on a rectangular base with canted corners. 2in. high. c.1835–50*
b. (right) Staffordshire King Charles spaniel seated on a shaped base decorated in pink. 1⅞in. high. c.1830–50.

COLOUR PLATE 152. *Pair of Staffordshire King Charles spaniels with Chinese-like faces, decorated with brown patches, each seated on a rectangular base with canted corners. 3in. high. Impressed 'T', which may denote a particular production batch. c.1835–50.*

COLOUR PLATE 153. *Staffordshire King Charles spaniel with brown feathered patches, together with a black and white puppy, lying recumbent on a deep base moulded with scrolls. 4⅝in. long. c.1835–50.*

COLOUR PLATE 154. *Staffordshire toy King Charles spaniel with black patches, $\frac{15}{16}$in. long, lying recumbent on a deep elaborate slightly tiered rectangular base with slanted edges, 1$\frac{7}{16}$in. long. c.1835–50. The same base was used to support a toy poodle similarly lying recumbent, but with raised rear.*

COLOUR PLATE 155. *Two Staffordshire groups, each consisting of a black and white King Charles spaniel and two puppies on a green cloth edged with orange, lying on top of a circular twin-handled wicker basket. 3½in. high. Possibly Dudson. c.1830–50. The reverse model would appear to be in a cat and two kittens on a cloth in a similar basket.*

Colour Plate 156. *Staffordshire black and white King Charles spaniel seated upright on a green and white stool with four white and gilt legs. 4⅛in. high. c.1830–50. The reverse model would appear to be a cat on a similar stool.*

Colour Plate 157. *Two King Charles spaniels, one with brown patches lying recumbent, the other with black patches jumping on top of it, on a cobalt-blue stool designed as an inkwell. 4⅛in. high. c.1840–50.*

Colour Plate 158. *Staffordshire group consisting of a King Charles spaniel with black markings, confronting a black and white tabby cat taking refuge in a tree stump on a mound base encrusted with flowers. 3¾in. high. c.1840–50.*

Christie's South Kensington

COLOUR PLATE 159. *Staffordshire group consisting of a King Charles spaniel or poodle and a cat, with a mouse dangling from its jaws, meeting beside a jug, on a green and white mound base edged with a gilt line. 3⅝in. long. c.1840–50.*
Christie's South Kensington

COLOUR PLATE 160. *Staffordshire brown and white King Charles spaniel and a reverse model, seated outside its moss-encrusted kennel, on a rocky rectangular base with rounded corners. 2⅝in. long. c.1840–50.*

Colour Plate 161. *Staffordshire white and brown King Charles spaniel lying outside its apricot kennel with pink roof, on an apricot rocky base, rectangular with rounded corners. 2½in. long. Impressed 'S', probably an identification mark of a particular factory batch. c.1840–50.*

Colour Plate 162. *Staffordshire group consisting of two King Charles spaniels, one standing (liver and white), the other lying down (black and white), outside an apricot kennel with pink roof encrusted at the base with moss, on a shaped triangular base. 3½in. wide. c.1840–50.*

COLOUR PLATE 163. *Group of two Staffordshire King Charles spaniels with brown patches, lying outside their pink-roofed kennel, on a pale-apricot triangular base. 2¼in. long. c.1840–50.*

COLOUR PLATE 164. *King Charles spaniel recumbent on a cushion base, in Parian. 7in. long. Unmarked. c.1850–70.*

GUN DOGS

Of pre-eminent importance to sportsmen in the period under discussion were setters and pointers. They acquired their respective names from their individual approaches to the game. Wood puts the matter as follows:

> As the pointers derive their name from their habits of standing still and pointing at any game which they may discover, so the SETTERS have earned their title from their custom of 'setting' or crouching when they perceive their game. In the olden days of sporting, the setter used always to drop as soon as it found the game, but at the present day the animal is in so far the imitator of the pointer, that it remains erect while marking down its game.[93]

Though completely different in appearance, these two breeds performed essentially the same function, and sportsmen were divided as to the superiority in the field, of the one as against the other. William Youatt said of them:

> The setter is more active than the pointer. He has greater spirit and strength. He will better stand continued hard work. He will generally take the water when necessary, and, retaining the character of the breed, is more companionable and attached. He loves his master for himself and not, like the pointer, for the pleasure he shares with him. His somewhat inferior scent, however, makes him too apt to run into his game, and he occasionally has a will of his own.[94]

SETTERS

The qualities of the setter are referred to by Thomas Bewick – its exquisite scent, its great speed, its wonderful perseverance, its sagacity and its caution. He concludes by quoting from Somervile:

> When autumn smiles, all beautious in decay,
> And paints each chequer'd grove with various hues,
> My Setter ranges in the new-shorn fields,
> His nose in air erect; from ridge to ridge
> Panting he bounds, his quarter'd ground divides
> In equal intervals, nor careless leaves
> One inch untry'd, at length the tainted gales
> His nostrils wide inhale; quick joy elates
> His beating heart, which, aw'd by discipline
> Severe, he dares not own, but cautious creeps
> Low-cow'ring, step by step; at last attains
> His proper distance; there he stops at once,
> And points with his instructive nose upon
> The trembling prey.[95]

An excellent engraving by J. Scott of an 'Old English Setter' appears in Daniel's *Rural Sports*, after a drawing by H.B. Chalon.

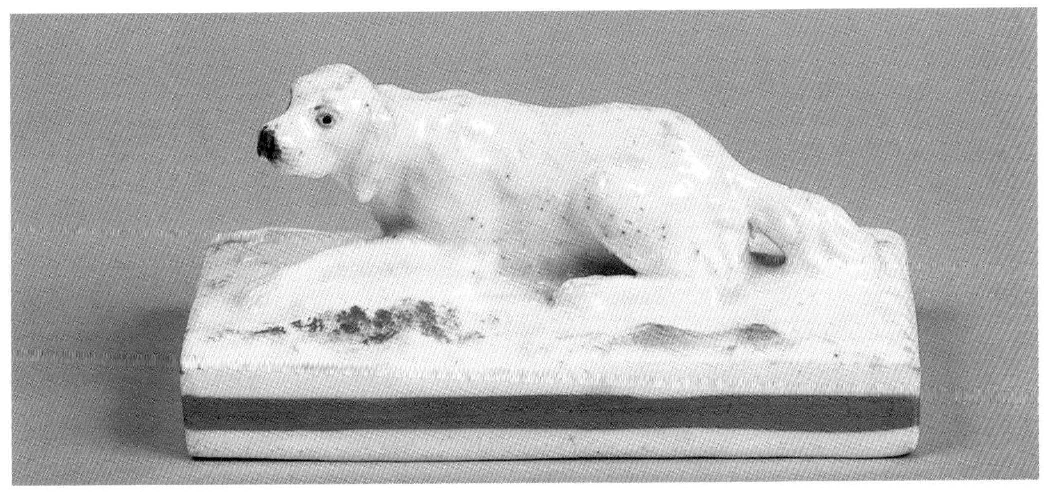

COLOUR PLATE 165. *Rockingham setter lying recumbent on a white and green rectangular base with a gilt line around the edges. 4¼in. long. Incised 'No 90' (an error for '94'). Cl. 1. 1826–30. Compare this with the examples of Colour Plates 126a and 166.*

Rockingham

The Rockingham factory produced three different models of a setter. The first (No 94) lies recumbent on a rectangular base, 4¼in. long. An example is shown in Colour Plate 126a and another in reverse in biscuit (Figure 9b). A pair appears in Colour Plate 166. The white example with black facial markings on a coloured base illustrated in Colour Plate 165 is erroneously incised 'No 90' instead of 'No 94'. The second setter model to

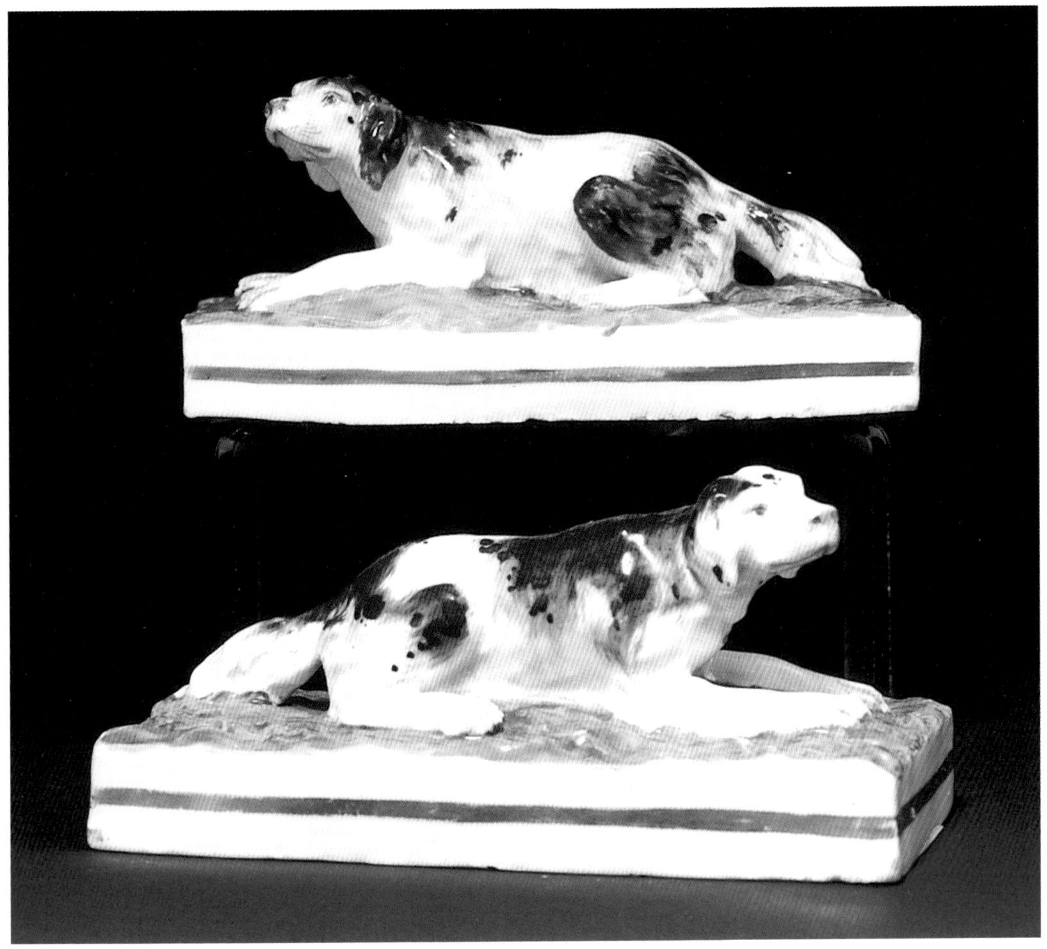

Colour Plate 166. *Pair of Rockingham setters, one enriched in iron red, the other with black patches, on rectangular bases edged with gilt lines, the surfaces painted in green and brown, 4¼in. long. 1826–30.*
Christie's South Kensington

COLOUR PLATE 167. *Rockingham setter in biscuit about to drink from a bowl, standing without support on a rectangular base. 3¼in. long. Incised 'No 84'. Impressed mark. 1826–30. For the underneath of the base see Figure 16.*

be turned out at Swinton – No 84 – assumes a standing position (incidentally without any support, in contrast to the terrier model No 89 – Colour Plate 220 and Figures 29 and 30) and is about to drink from a bowl.[96] An example in biscuit, so far a unique survivor, is shown in Colour Plate 167. The base of the animal (Figure 16) demonstrates the form of construction used on Rockingham (and for that matter, contemporary Derby and Minton) animals. The Rockingham impressed mark and the incised model number can also be seen.

The third Rockingham model of a setter – No 96 – is illustrated in Colour Plate 168. It stands only 1¾in. high.

FIGURE 16. *Base of the dog of Colour Plate 167. Like the contemporary Derby and Minton models, it is closed-in save for a centrally located hole. It is incised with the model number, and is impressed with the full Griffin mark appropriate to the period 1826–30.*

COLOUR PLATE 168. *Rockingham toy setter with a gilt collar seated on an oval mound base. 1¾in. high. Incised 'No 96'. Cl. 1. 1826–30.*

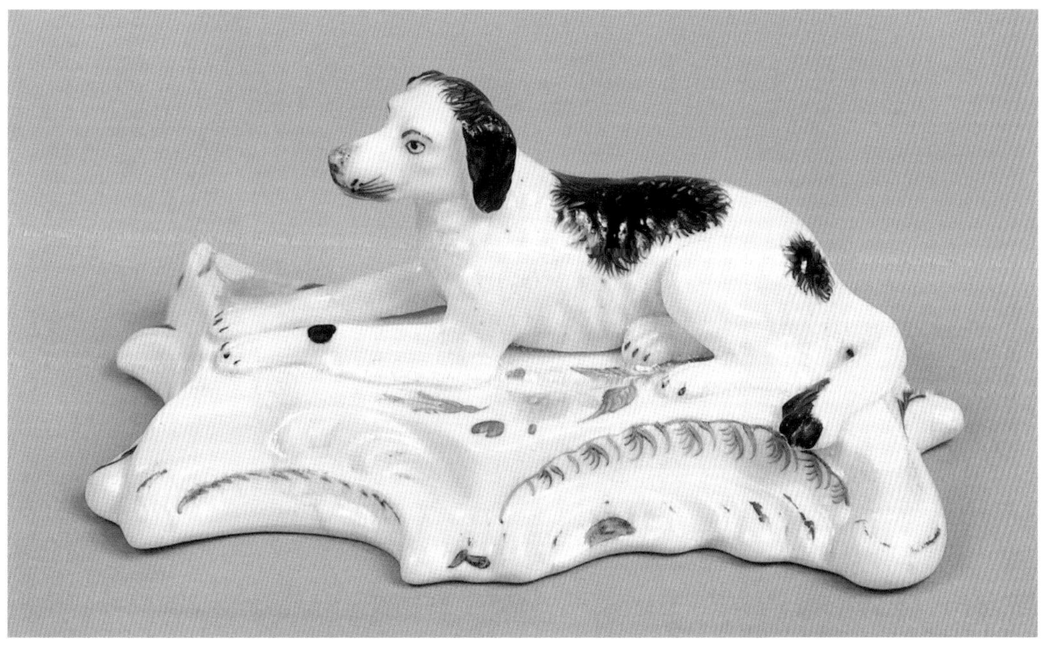

COLOUR PLATE 169. *Derby setter with black patches lying recumbent on a shaped rectangular base moulded with elaborate scrolling, painted with pink roses and foliage. 5in. long. c.1835–46.*

Derby

The large setter shown in Figure 17 (right) with its nose close to the ground sniffing the scent, standing on a rocky base (the companion of which is a pointer), was made at Derby, but although it was undoubtedly produced during the nineteenth century,[97] it would appear to have been an eighteenth century model. According to Haslem, the original model was the work of William Coffee made during the 1790s.

The setter illustrated in Colour Plate 170a is seemingly of Derby origin. It has the base typical of the factory, i.e. closed-in save for a centrally located hole (Colour Plate 170b). Another example similarly decorated is shown in Colour Plate 169. The reverse model

FIGURE 17. *Derby pointer (left) and companion setter (right) in natural colours, the pointer trotting, the setter with its nose to the ground. 6½in. long. Late eighteenth or early nineteenth century.*

Grosvenor Antiques Ltd. and Mary Wise Antiques.

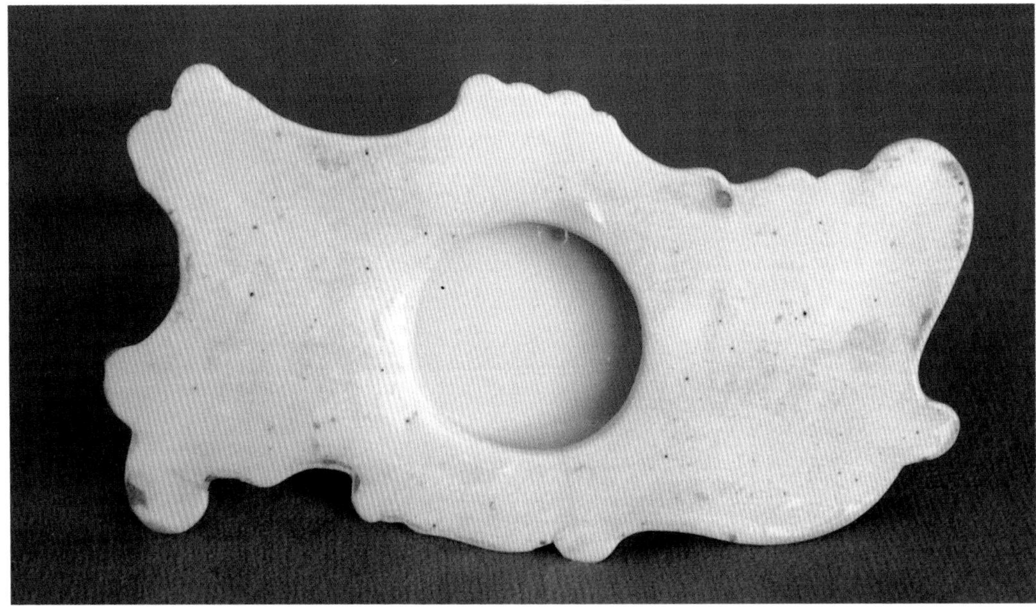

COLOUR PLATE 170. *a. (above). Derby setter with black patches lying recumbent on a shaped rectangular base moulded with elaborate scrolling, painted with pink roses and foliage. 5in. long. c.1835–46.*
b. (right). The underneath of the base, indicating a Derby origin. The Staffordshire version is not closed-in. The same underneath of the base is found in the case of the pointers of Colour Plate 188.

would seem to be a pointer. Two examples of a pointer on the same type of base are shown in Colour Plate 188. (Each, like the corresponding setter, is painted with pink roses, but in addition, it has forget-me-nots.) However, the pointer is not an exact replica in reverse of the setter. For whereas the former is poised to rise – the body is off the ground and all four legs are in position to enable the animal to move off at once – the setter is lying fully recumbent with one of its back legs under its body.

Grainger Lee & Co., Worcester

A setter and a pointer, in reverse to each other, appear in the Grainger Lee pattern book. Although a porcelain example of the pointer is recorded (Colour Plate 190), no porcelain example of the setter has so far come to light.

COLOUR PLATE 171. *Minton setter in biscuit lying recumbent on a tasselled cushion. 4½in. long. c.1831–40.*

Minton

The biscuit setter shown in Colour Plate 171 emanates from the Minton factory; the underneath of the base is typical of the factory, i.e. it is closed-in save for a centrally located hole. In addition, the dog lies on the same tasselled cushion base found in conjunction with the factory's King Charles spaniels (the one recumbent, Colour Plate 128, and the other begging), two different poodle models (the one originally with a basket, Colour Plate 54, the other without a basket), the recumbent pug (Colour Plate 34), the recumbent greyhound (Colour Plate 4) and the 'Russian dog'. Admittedly there is no illustration in the factory drawing book of a setter on a tasselled cushion or, for that matter, of a setter of any kind, but notwithstanding its omission from the book (it may be one of the non-illustrated items simply described as 'Dog'), it is clearly a product of the factory. What is surprising, however, is that the dog is recumbent on a tasselled cushion, a base wholly appropriate to a lap-dog, but quite unsuited for a sporting dog such as a setter.

It is of particular interest, then, to see in Colour Plate 172 the same dog, but on a totally different base, this time rectangular in form, 4⅛in. long, i.e. some ⅜in. shorter than the base of the dog of Colour Plate 171. The underneath is identical to that of the Minton tasselled cushion base and the Rockingham and Derby animal bases, i.e. flat and closed-in save for a small centrally located hole. The base is, however, heavier than the bases associated with Rockingham and Derby models, and is decorated in a style characteristic of the Minton artists – note the use of two single gilt lines running around the edges of the base enclosing a gilt pattern.[98] More importantly, the top and bottom, where the two gilt lines appear, are slightly raised, as also is the distinctive scrolling picked out in gold. This raised moulding appears in identical form on the oval base of the Newfoundland dog shown in illustration Nos 25 and 26 of the factory drawing book. The base appearing in Colour Plate 172 seems more appropriate for a setter than

COLOUR PLATE 172. *Minton black and white setter lying recumbent on a rectangular base edged with two gilt lines enclosing a raised scroll moulding 4⅛in.long. c.1831–40. This is the same model as that of Colour Plate 171, but with a different base. The reverse is the pointer of Colour Plate 192.*

the tasselled cushion version. Presumably, in the case of the latter base, the repairer, in the exercise of artistic licence, departed from reality simply to produce a pleasing composition. It is interesting to note that a well-known Ralph Wood pottery model of a setter was also made to sit on a cushion base,[99] and that the records of the Chamberlain factory reveal that even stags were sometimes modelled on cushions.

Illustration No 119 in the drawing book shows a setter sitting upright on a high mound base. The model is in fact 7in. high in all and was later replaced in Parian by a 'Persian Greyhound' (Colour Plate 215).

Copeland & Garrett

The printed factory mark appears under the base of a large Copeland & Garrett setter recumbent on a green rectangular base, 8in. by 4in.[100] Presumably, there was once a companion pointer (or possibly setter) in reverse.

COLOUR PLATE 173. *Brown and white setter lying recumbent on a green rectangular base with slanting edges. 4½in. long. Possibly Davenport. c.1830–50. The animal is heavy in weight and richly gilded, features of the Davenport factory.*

Colour Plate 174. *Samuel Alcock black and white setter lying recumbent on a yellow shaped base with elaborate scrolling. 5in. long. Impressed '13'. c.1835–50.*

Davenport

Possibly from the Davenport factory is the setter with liver markings shown in Colour Plate 173. The quality of the modelling and the thickness of the gilding suggest at least the possibility of a Davenport attribution.

Samuel Alcock

The setter shown in Colour Plate 174 comes from the Samuel Alcock factory. It is similar in modelling to the Derby version illustrated in Colour Plates 169 and 170. It is impressed '13' and its companion model, a pointer, is similarly numbered. In the case of some pairs, the setter is made to look in the opposite direction to that faced by the example of Colour Plate 174, and the companion pointer is reversed accordingly.

In view of the fact that the setter of Colour Plate 174 is impressed '13',[101] the model must have come into existence before the foundation stone of the new factory was laid in April 1839, for the models buried under the foundation stone carry later numbers, including 86 or 98 (the correct number depends on which way up the object was meant to be viewed). It would seem reasonable then, to date the origin of the model to around 1837 or a little before and, if it was based on a pre-existing Derby version, it would seem probable that the latter was first made around 1835. It is unlikely there would be any significant gap between the date when the Derby model first appeared and the date when it was subsequently copied by Samuel Alcock.

The dog illustrated in Colour Plate 175 would appear to have a Samuel Alcock origin, notwithstanding it is not impressed with a number. The base is similar to, but not so sharply moulded, as that which supports the factory's saluki (No 311) shown in Colour Plate 214. The breed is not easy to identify – several possibilities suggest themselves – but on balance it seems that the factory intended it to represent a seated setter.

Colour Plate 175. *Setter with brown patches, seated upright, on a flat mound base with rocky sides. 3⅞in. high. Probably Samuel Alcock. c.1840–50. Five black dots are painted under the base. This model is also recorded on a cobalt-blue base.*

Unidentified Staffordshire Factories

The setters of Colour Plates 178 and 179 are from the same factory, and are in fact companion models. That this is so is demonstrated by the pair of dogs illustrated in Colour Plate 180. One of them is the same model that appears in Colour Plate 178, the other the same model seen in Colour Plate 179. However, a reverse model of Colour Plate 178 has been recorded, which suggests that the factory in effect produced three different pairs of setters, namely the model of Colour Plate 178 as a pair, the model of Colour Plate 179 as a pair and a combination of these models to make the pair shown in Colour Plate 180. There is nothing to indicate that any of these models was paired with a pointer.

Another Staffordshire setter is seen in Colour Plate 177. It lies recumbent on an elaborately scrolled base, 4⅞in. long, similar to that of the Derby setter of Colour Plates

Colour Plate 176. *Staffordshire setter with black and grey markings lying recumbent on a green shaped rectangular base moulded with elaborate scrolling. 4⅞in. long. c.1835–50. Compare Colour Plate 177.*
Christie's South Kensington

Colour Plate 177. *Staffordshire setter lying on a light-blue shaped rectangular base with elaborate scrolling. 4⅞in. long. c.1835–50. Note the unusual light-blue decoration. In a way typical of Staffordshire products, the underneath of the base is left open. Compare Colour Plate 176.*

COLOUR PLATE 178. *Staffordshire black and white setter, with its head turned back and looking upwards, lying recumbent on a cobalt-blue rectangular base edged in white and gold. 4⅝in. long. c.1830–50. Compare the pair in Colour Plate 180.*

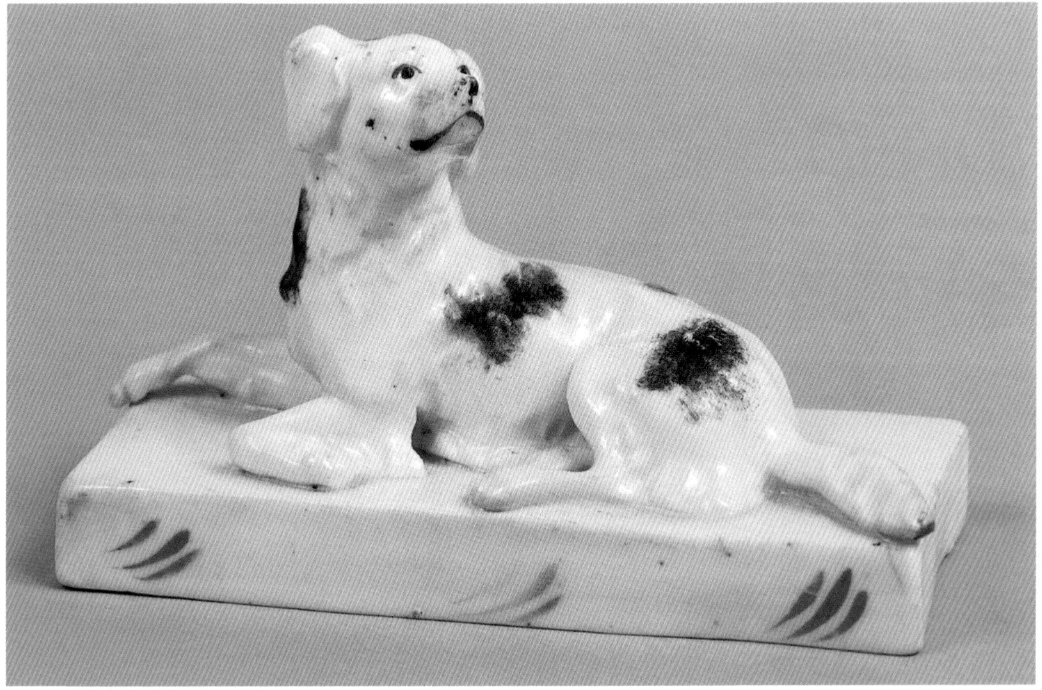

COLOUR PLATE 179. *Staffordshire setter, with chestnut brown patches, its head turned back and looking upwards, its right front paw and tail slightly overhanging the rectangular base on which it is lying recumbent, the front edge of the base splashed with gold. 4¾in. long. c.1830–50. This is the companion model to the setter of Colour Plate 178. Compare with the pair in Colour Plate 180.*

169 and 170. An unusual feature is the light-blue ground colour covering the top of the base. Another example of this model appears in Colour Plate 176. This time the dog, decorated with black and grey markings, lies on a green base. The reverse model is normally a pointer. However, the factory was not always consistent. A case is recorded where the companion model was another setter in reverse.

The remaining Staffordshire setters illustrated here are sufficiently described in the relevant captions as not to require further comment.

Colour Plate 180. *Pair of Staffordshire setters, black and white, each with head turned back and looking upwards, lying recumbent on a cobalt-blue rectangular base edged in white and gold. 4½in. long. 1830–50. Compare with Colour Plates 178 and 179.*

Colour Plate 181. *Staffordshire black and white recumbent setter licking its recumbent puppy outside a kennel in the form of a house, on a green shaped base. 4⅝in. long. c.1840–50.*

COLOUR PLATE 182. *Two Staffordshire toy setters together with a toy pointer, each with liver markings, standing on a rocky pad base edged with a continuous gilt line. 1¾in. long. c.1835–50. The smooth thin tail of the pointer contrasting with the fluffy tail of the setters is the only practical feature distinguishing one model from the other.*

COLOUR PLATE 183. *Pair of Staffordshire toy groups, consisting of a black and white pointer with a man and a brown and white setter with a lady. 4in. high. c.1835–50.*

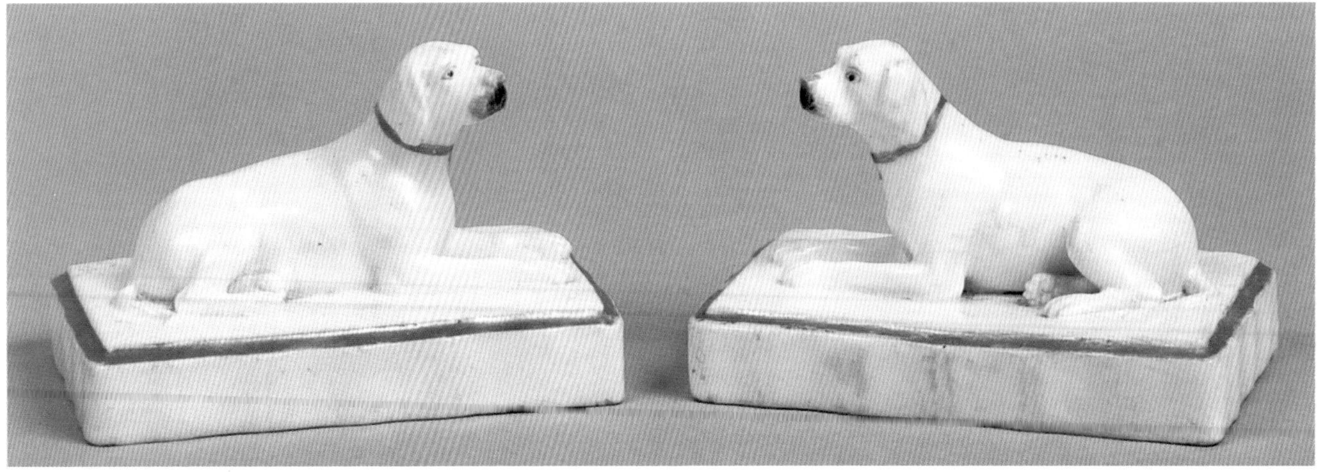

COLOUR PLATE 184. *Pair of Rockingham white and gilt pointers, a dog and a bitch, each lying recumbent, head raised, on a flat rectangular base with pinched sections and decorated with a continuous gilt line. 3¼in. long. Incised 'No 92'. Cl. 1. 1826–30.*

POINTERS

The Spanish pointer was brought to this country from Spain in the 1650s, and was probably reintroduced after the Treaty of Utrecht in 1713. However, it was too slow to satisfy the needs of the nineteenth century sportsman, and was developed by cross-breeding into what became known as the 'English pointer'. The latter, while retaining the 'nose' of the former, proved to be a tireless hunter, a good stayer and swift enough to run down a leveret. Examples of English pointers in the form of the celebrated dog 'Dash' and the pair 'Pluto and Juno' appear in Daniel's *Rural Sports*. They have lost the heavy shoulders and short muzzle of the original Spanish pointer. Daniel also illustrates

FIGURE 18. *Rockingham Spanish pointer bitch, white and gilt, trotting with tree support on a rocky base. 4½in. long. Incised 'No 93'. Impressed mark. After George Stubbs. 1826–30. Presumably there was a companion dog in reverse.* T.A. Lockett, Esq.

FIGURE 19. *Rockingham white and gilt pointer, looking upwards, seated on an oval base. 3in. high. Incised 'No 101'. Impressed mark. 1826–30. For a white and gilt bitch see Colour Plate 186b, and for a pair in colour see Colour Plate 185.* Mr. and Mrs. Dunnington

an interesting engraving by J. Scott of a 'Spanish Pointer' after a painting by George Stubbs'. Another engraving was executed by Bewick in reverse.

COLOUR PLATE 185. *Pair of Rockingham pointers, looking upwards, one a dog, the other a bitch, each decorated with dark indigo and fawn patches, seated on an oval puce base. 2¾in. high. Incised 'No 101'. Cl. 2. 1826–30. See also Colour Plate 186b and Figure 19.*

Rockingham

The Rockingham animal illustrated in Figure 18 (No 93) would appear to be a Spanish pointer bitch – after the painting by George Stubbs. It presumably had a dog of the same breed as a companion in reverse.

The Rockingham factory also produced two further pairs of pointers (Nos 92 and 101), illustrated respectively in Colour Plate 184 and Colour Plates 185, 186b and Figure 19. Model No 101 may well have been based on the Derby pointers of Colour Plate 186a.

Derby

The Derby pointer referred to above holds its head in a position similar to that of the pointer that accompanies Gainsborough's painting of Mr. and Mrs.

COLOUR PLATE 186. *a. (left). Two grey and white Derby pointers, each looking upwards and seated on a green oval base. 2½in. high. c.1830.*
b. (right). Rockingham white and gilt pointer bitch, looking upwards, seated on an oval base. 2¾in. high. Incised No 101. 1826–30. For a white and gilt dog see Figure 19.

COLOUR PLATE 187. *Derby pointer with a gilt collar standing with tree stump support on a deep oval base in green edged with a gilt band. 2⅛in. high. Factory mark in iron red. c.1830.*
Christie's South Kensington

Andrews,[102] and it would seem that this dog is to be identified with:

	Enamelled and gilt
Dogs from the Dresden shepherd, each	1s 0d

included by Haslem in his list of Bow and Chelsea models.[103] The dog that accompanies the Dresden Shepherd (the group is No 55 in Haslem's general list) was produced as an independent model in the eighteenth century.[104] The dogs in Colour Plate 186a are nineteenth century examples.

An unusual feature of the pointers of Colour Plate 188 is the fine painting of pink roses and forget-me-nots on the top of the base. Compare the Setters of Colour Plates 169 and 170.[105]

It is not easy to say whether the dog of Colour Plate 187 is a pointer or a foxhound. On balance I think it more likely that a pointer was intended. The animal undoubtedly comes from the Derby factory, as it bears the factory mark in iron-red. The form of the base is identical to that of the unmarked greyhounds of Colour Plate 1 and Figure 3, and accordingly puts their attribution to Derby beyond dispute.

Mention should also be made of the pointer that is the companion of the setter in Figure 17 (p.105).

COLOUR PLATE 188. *Two Derby pointers, one with black, the other with liver markings, each lying recumbent on a shaped rectangular base moulded with elaborate scrolling and painted with forget-me-nots and pink roses. 5in. long. c.1835–46.*

COLOUR PLATE 189. *Chamberlain Worcester toy pointer standing with tree support on a green base with white and gilt leaves. 2in. long. Impressed 'CHAMBERLAINS' in capitals under the base, which is flat and completely closed-in. c.1847–52.*

Chamberlain Worcester

A toy pointer from the Chamberlain Worcester factory is illustrated in Colour Plate 189.[106]

Grainger Lee & Co., Worcester

An example (hitherto unrecorded) of the trotting pointer which appears in the factory pattern book is to be seen in Colour Plate 190. Miraculously, particularly in view of the thin erect tail, it has survived in perfect condition and the gilding is quite unrubbed. Doubtless it owes its unblemished state to its having been for most of its existence under a glass dome. It should be noted that in the case of this particular model, unlike the Minton pointer of Colour Plate 191 and the Rockingham hound of Colour Plate 199, the animal has no tree support, a considerable technical achievement on the part of the factory.[107]

COLOUR PLATE 190. *Grainger Lee white and gilt pointer in a trotting position on a white and gilt mound base, with erect tail and raised right leg bent back. 4¾in. long. Mark: 'GRAINGER LEE & CO, WORCESTER' lightly impressed. 1820–37.*

Colour Plate 191.
Minton pointer, with black patches, trotting beside a supporting tree, on a green rocky mound base. 3½in. long. Model No 31. c.1831–40.

Colour Plate 192.
Minton pointer with brown patches lying recumbent on a rectangular base decorated in green with brown stippling, edged with two gilt lines enclosing a raised scroll moulding. 4¼in. long. c.1831–40. This is the reverse model to the setter of Colour Plate 172.

Minton

Model No 31 in the factory list is represented by a trotting pointer, and an example is shown in Colour Plate 191. Another pointer model executed by the factory is illustrated in Colour Plate 192. It does not appear in the drawing book. It is the reverse of the setter of Colour Plate 172, although differently decorated. Presumably, the setter lying on a tasselled cushion base, shown in Colour Plate 171, also had as a companion model a pointer in reverse, but so far no example is recorded [108] As with the setter, the pointer does not appear in the factory drawing book. Such is the case with certain other Minton animals.

COLOUR PLATE 193. *Samuel Alcock liver and white pointer trotting beside a supporting tree on an oval rocky base decorated in green. 6¼in. long. Impressed '108'. c.1840–50.*

Samuel Alcock

The Samuel Alcock factory was responsible for at least two pointer models. One of them, trotting beside a tree support on an oval base (impressed '108'), is shown in Colour Plate 193. The other version, No13, is the reverse of the setter appearing in Colour Plate 174.[109]

Unidentified Staffordshire Factories

Pointers were produced by various Staffordshire factories operating during the period 1830–50. A fine example, accompanied by three puppies, in a wicker basket is illustrated in Colour Plate 195 and Figure 20.[110] The reverse model would appear to be a cat and three kittens in a similar basket. The connection would seem somewhat strange in view of the disparity in size between the *real* animals. Some degree of artistic licence would appear to have been in operation. It is noteworthy that the pointer and three puppies group is (subject of course to the substitution of a wicker basket for the scrolled base) essentially the same as the poodle and three puppies of Colour Plate 88. The only significant difference is that, in the case of the latter group, the bitch is encrusted with porcelain granules and the puppies lightly sprayed with a porcelain pebble-dash finish to simulate wool.

In discussing Staffordshire setters (Colour Plates 176 and 177), reference was made to a type of pointer that is the reverse model. An example of a pointer on such a base is illustrated in Colour Plate 194.

Figure 20. *Staffordshire group of a pointer with three puppies, in a cobalt-blue rectangular wicker basket with rounded corners and twin-handles. 4½in. high. Possibly Dudson. c.1830–50. Compare the group of Colour Plate 195.* Sotheby's

COLOUR PLATE 194. *Staffordshire pointer with liver-red patches lying recumbent on a shaped rectangular base in pink moulded with elaborate scrolling in white and gold. 5in. long. c.1835–50.*
Christie's South Kensington

COLOUR PLATE 195. *Staffordshire black and white pointer seated with three puppies in a straw-lined rectangular green wicker-work basket with twin handles, with rounded corners. 4¼in. high. Marked in red '112'. Possibly Dudson. c.1830–50. Compare the example in Figure 20.*

Models of the following breeds are, on the whole, rarely seen, and it seems reasonable to assume that they were produced less frequently and in limited quantities. For these reasons the attribution of models to factories of manufacture is dealt with in a more compact form than is given to the preceding breed models and factories of manufacture.

GREAT DANES/DANISH DOGS

As its name suggests, the Great Dane was originally imported into this country from Denmark. It was used to accompany and guard carriages. By the end of the eighteenth century the breed appeared in three different colours, fawn, harlequin, and a bluish-grey marbled with black. Taplin in *The Sportsman's Cabinet* writes of the dog:

> The majestic and commanding aspect, bold muscular action, and elegant carriage of this dog would recommend him to notice, had he not other useful properties or points of attraction. Those he has already in possession we observe honoured in adding to the splendid pomp and magnificent retinues of the noble, wealthy and independent, before whose emblazoned vehicles he trots or gallops with a degree of dignity denoting no small consciousness of the patronage he is under and the state of grandeur he is selected to precede and support.

The dog illustrated in Figure 21 would appear to be a Great Dane. It comes from the Grainger Lee factory, although it is not represented in the factory's pattern book. Great Dane models are rare.

FIGURE 21. *Grainger Lee Great Dane, white and gilt, lying recumbent on a rocky base. 4¾in. long. Impressed with the factory mark. 1820–37.* The Museum of Worcester Porcelain

COLOUR PLATE 196. *Pair of Staffordshire black-spotted Dalmatians, each seated on a cobalt-blue mound base. 6¼in. high. c.1840–50.* John Read Antiques

DALMATIANS

Certain Staffordshire factories turned out Dalmatians often lying recumbent on a cobalt-blue base. The Dalmatian, albeit smaller than the Great Dane, performed essentially the same function as the latter; that is to say, it ran with and protected carriages and their contents. An interesting pair of Staffordshire Dalmatians, seated on cobalt-blue bases, are illustrated in Colour Plate 196.

The Samuel Alcock factory is known to have produced a pair of Dalmatians impressed '310'. Each sits upright on a mound base, 2¾in. high in all. The only known pair are on a yellow base.

Seemingly, a further model is to be attributed to the Samuel Alcock factory. For there is a reference to: 'A Rockingham [on no footing could it be Rockingham] Figure of a Dalmatian, sleepily emerging from his kennel surrounded by a border of green moss, gilt line-edged base, 2¼in. *impressed numeral* 142'.[111]

Colour Plate 197.
Rockingham mastiff, with tongue hanging out, decorated with ochre patches, lying recumbent on a rocky base flecked with gold. 4⅞in. long. Incised 'No 90'. Cl. 2. Impressed mark.

MASTIFFS

The mastiff, if not native to this country, has certainly been here since at least the middle ages. Initially, it was used as a guard dog, and very effective it was in this capacity. In 1586 William Harrison said of it in *The Description of England*:

> The Mastiff is a huge, stubborn, ugly and impetuous hound, with a large frame that renders it slow of movement. Its natural savagery is increased by the course of training to which it is submitted, being pitted against bears, bulls or lions, if the latter could be found.

Apart from being a guard dog the mastiff was used for bull- and bear-baiting, but eventually it was replaced for this purpose by the bulldog.

It is said of the mastiff that, once the boundaries of its master's property have been shown to it, it will not wander outside them. It was, during our period, often chained

Colour Plate 198.
Pair of Samuel Alcock mastiffs, black and white, each lying on a yellow rocky base, one with its tongue hanging out. 5½in. long. Impressed '305'. c.1840–50.

by day, but left free to roam at night in performance of its duties as a guard dog.[112]

Notwithstanding the qualities of the mastiff as a fighting or guard dog – qualities reflected in the appearance given to the animal in the porcelain models that have so far come to light – there was a kinder nature to be found in the breed. Sydenham Edwards speaks of this in his *Cynographia Britannica*:

> What the Lion is to the cat, the mastiff is to the dog, the noblest of the family; he stands alone and all others sink before him. His courage does not exceed his temper and generosity, and in the attachment he equals the kindest of his race. His docility is perfect: the teasing of the smaller kinds will hardly provoke him to resent, and I have seen him down with his paw the terrier or the cur that has bit him without offering further injury. In a family he will permit the children to play with him, and suffer all their pranks without offence.

The gentler version of the mastiff appears, for example, in the picture by Anthony Van Dyck of 'The Children of Charles 1', c.1630.[113] However, all the porcelain representations so far recorded portray the animal in its aggressive guise.

Illustrated here are the Rockingham version (Colour Plate 197) and a pair from the Samuel Alcock factory (Colour Plate 198).

FOXHOUNDS

By the end of the eighteenth century the foxhound, which had started off very much a mongrel, had become the purest breed then existing. A fine pair were painted by George Stubbs.[114] Another pair by Reinagle, feature in *The Sportsman's Cabinet*. The qualities sought of a foxhound were a wide chest, a broad back, straight legs, a small head, a thin neck and a bushy tail.

Foxhounds were not represented in porcelain on any significant scale. This is perhaps

Colour Plate 199. *Rockingham white and gilt foxhound bitch standing with tree support on a mound base. 4⅝in. long. Incised 'No 85'. Cl. 1. 1826–30.*

COLOUR PLATE 200. *Two Rockingham white and gilt toy foxhounds seated, one 1⅜in. high, incised 'No 74'; the other 1⅛in. high, incised 'No 71'. Cl. 1. 1826–30.*

somewhat surprising in view of their large numbers and importance to the hunting and agricultural community. In particular, one would have expected the Staffordshire factories to have turned them out in profusion. But such is not the case.

However, some models do exist. Two toy dogs produced at Swinton, Nos 71 and 74, (Colour Plate 200) appear to be foxhounds. They are extremely small, being only 1⅛in. and 1⅜in. high respectively.

In addition, the Rockingham factory turned out a much larger hound in the form of the animal illustrated in Colour Plate 199 (No 85). As it is a bitch, there was presumably a companion dog in reverse, although so far no example has surfaced.

No foxhound appears to have been produced by the Derby factory in Nottingham Road, but the Derby King Street factory did manufacture such a model. It is illustrated

COLOUR PLATE 201. *White-glazed foxhound sniffing, from the King Street Derby factory. 3½in. long. Sampson Hancock mark in blue. Later nineteenth century.*

here in Colour Plate 201. The Chamberlain Worcester factory also modelled a hound. One such on a green stepped base is shown in Colour Plate 202. This same model is also recorded on a pink base. A Parian group comprising a hound feeding or drinking from a dish held by a seated girl was produced by the Samuel Alcock factory. An example with the factory mark is shown in Battie.[115]

Vivian illustrates a pair of foxhounds[116] which she erroneously calls Rockingham. They were in fact from Staffordshire. A similar pair are illustrated in Colour Plate 203. The only difference is that, whereas the former pair sat on rocky cobalt-blue bases, the latter are supported on smooth white bases. (These models also appear in pottery.) A further example of the straight-backed hound can be seen in Colour Plate 204. An interesting feature is the three-tone rocky base inscribed underneath '141' in red. It may be that these foxhounds came from the Dudson factory.[117]

It is to be noted that the straight-backed foxhound of Colour Plates 203 and 204 is the same dog with minor variations, to accommodate the change in breed, as the poodle bitch of Colour Plates 88 and 89, and the pointer bitch of Colour Plate 195 and Figure 20. The arch-backed foxhound corresponds to the arch-backed poodle referred to at p.65.

COLOUR PLATE 202. *Chamberlain Worcester foxhound seated on a green stepped rectangular base with canted corners. 2⅝in. high. c.1820–40.*

COLOUR PLATE 203. *Pair of Staffordshire foxhounds with brown patches, chained, one with straight back, the other arched, each seated on a mound base. 4¼in. and 4in. high respectively. Possibly Dudson. c.1830–50. The straight-backed dog is the same model as that of Colour Plate 204, although seated on a different base. Compare the poodle of Colour Plates 88 and 89 and the pointer of Colour Plate 195 and Figure 20.*

COLOUR PLATE 204. *Staffordshire foxhound with straight back and turned head, sitting chained on a rocky base decorated in brown, green and yellow. 4in. high. Inscribed under the base '141' in red. Possibly Dudson. c.1830–50.*

COLOUR PLATE 205. *Rockingham standing shepherd with a shepherd's dog with brown patches on a white and gilt rocky base. 8½in. high. Incised 'No 4'. Impressed mark. 1826–30.*

COLOUR PLATE 206. *Rockingham standing shepherd with a Continental dog at his feet. 7¼in. high. Incised 'No 4'. Red Griffin mark. 1826–30. This group, which is an earlier version of that in Colour Plate 205, is a copy of a Bow group, which is in turn based on the Meissen.*

SHEPHERD'S DOGS/SHEEPDOGS

Wood depicts the sheepdog (described more aptly as 'the shepherd's dog') saying of it:

> As the Sheep-dog is constantly exposed to the weather, it needs the protection of a very thick and closely-set fur, which, in this Dog, is rather woolly in its character, and is especially heavy about the neck and breast . . . The muzzle of this Dog is sharp, its head is of moderate size, its eyes are very bright and intelligent, as might be expected in an animal of so much sagacity and ready resource in time of need. Its feet are strongly made, and sufficiently well protected to ensure severe

> work among the harsh stems of the heather on the hills, or the sharply-cutting stones of the high road. Probably, on account of its constant exercise in the open air, and the hardy manner in which it is brought up, the Sheep-dog is perhaps the most untiring of our domesticated animals . . . As a general rule, the Sheep-dog cares very little for anyone but his master, and so far from courting the notice or caresses of a stranger will coldly withdraw from them, and keeps his distance. Even with other Dogs he rarely makes companionship, contenting himself with the society of his master alone.[110]

The dog which accompanies the shepherd of Rockingham model No 4 (second version) illustrated in Colour Plate 205, and the shepherd of model No 58 shown in Figure 22 (p.130) is, as we would expect, an excellent model of a sheepdog. Surprisingly, it seems never to appear separately from the group. The same is true of the Continental sheepdog that accompanies the first version of the Rockingham Model No 4 illustrated in Colour Plate 206.

What would appear to be a sheepdog from the Derby factory is illustrated in Figure 23 (p.130). An example of a Staffordshire sheepdog is shown together with a reclining boy in Colour Plate 207.

COLOUR PLATE 207. *Staffordshire rustic group consisting of a reclining boy with a black and white shepherd's dog lying beside him, its front paw in his hand, on a two-tier oval base with scrolled edges picked out in gold. 6in. long. c.1840–50. The companion model in reverse is a reclining girl with a goat.*

FIGURE 22. *Rockingham shepherd with shepherd's dog and sheep in biscuit. 7¼in. high. Incised 'No 58'. Impressed mark. 1826–30.*
John Gallagher, Esq.

It is interesting to note that in the case of certain eighteenth century shepherd and dog groups, where the model is taken from a Meissen original, the dog wears a spiked collar.[119] On the Continent, in countries where the flock was still exposed to the attack of the wolf, the dog was protected in this way, for it was used to guard the flock, not to drive it. The shepherd would control the direction of the flock by the use of a 'tame wether accustomed to feed from his hands. The favourite, however distant, obeys his call, and the rest follow'.[120] An alternative throat protection is worn by the dog in the Rockingham group of Colour Plate 206.

FIGURE 23. *Derby shepherd's dog, with black patches, seated on a green rocky mound base. 2½in. high. c.1830.* Christie's South Kensington

COLOUR PLATE 208. *Grainger Lee white and gilt Indian Hare dog standing on a rocky rectangular base flecked with gold. 4¾in. long. Mark: 'GRAINGER LEE & CO WORCESTER', lightly impressed. 1820–37. Compare the example in Figure 24.*

FIGURE 24. *Grainger Lee Indian Hare dog with black markings standing on a rocky rectangular base. 5⅛in. long. Impressed with the factory mark. 1820–37. Compare the dog of Colour Plate 208.*
The Museum of Worcester Porcelain

INDIAN HARE DOGS

The Grainger Lee dog illustrated in Colour Plate 208 is an Indian Hare Dog. Another example, somewhat larger in size, is in the Dyson Perrins Museum (Figure 24). The

COLOUR PLATE 209. *Grainger Lee white and gilt Indian Hare dog lying recumbent, head raised, on a scrolled mound base, 4⅝in. long. Impressed 'GRAINGER LEE & CO WORCESTER'. 1820–37. Compare the dog of Figure 25.*

model appears in the factory pattern book together with its reverse. The factory also produced the model lying down. One version with head raised[121] is illustrated in Colour Plate 209 and Figure 25, while the companion model in reverse is shown in Figure 26. Interestingly, the recumbent models do not appear in the pattern book, but such absence is equally true of other Grainger Lee models.

That the dog is to be identified as an Indian Hare Dog can be established by the reference to this particular breed in the factory's records of its models[122] and the correspondence between the animals here illustrated, and the illustration of 'A Hare Indian dog of a collie type' in Ash. Moreover, this particular breed had been exhibited since 1827/28 in the Zoological Gardens in Regent's Park, London, and would, at the time it was represented in porcelain by the Grainger Lee factory, have been a topical novelty. Ash writes of it as follows:

> Another of the supposed wild dogs is the Hare Indian dog (*canis lagopus*), a variety once found in the possession of the tribes of Indians frequenting the borders of the Great Bear Lake and the banks of the Mackenzie . . . The Hare Indian dog, judging from illustrations, was of the present-day collie type but smaller. A pair of these dogs were imported into England and placed in the Zoological Gardens, where they bred two litters, and were found to be very gentle, lively, and familiar, but not without certain wildness. One, permitted his liberty, was not retaken except with considerable trouble. They were soon gained over by kindness and were fond of being caressed. When petted, they rubbed their backs against the hand in the manner of cats. They did not tamely submit to punishment and were very mindful of injuries. If irritated, they howled like wolves, but did not then attempt to bark; but if surprised and interested by some unusual object, they

FIGURE 25. *Grainger Lee Indian hare dog in enamel colours lying recumbent, head raised. 4⅝in. long. Impressed 'GRAINGER LEE & CO WORCESTER'. 1820–37. Compare the dog of Colour Plate 209.* Christie's

would make a singular attempt at barking commencing with a kind of growl, which was not, however, unpleasant, and ending in a prolonged howl. The voice was very much like that of the prairie wolf. In their own country they frequently fell victims to larger dogs which devoured them. In proportion to their size they possessed great muscular strength and perseverance.[123]

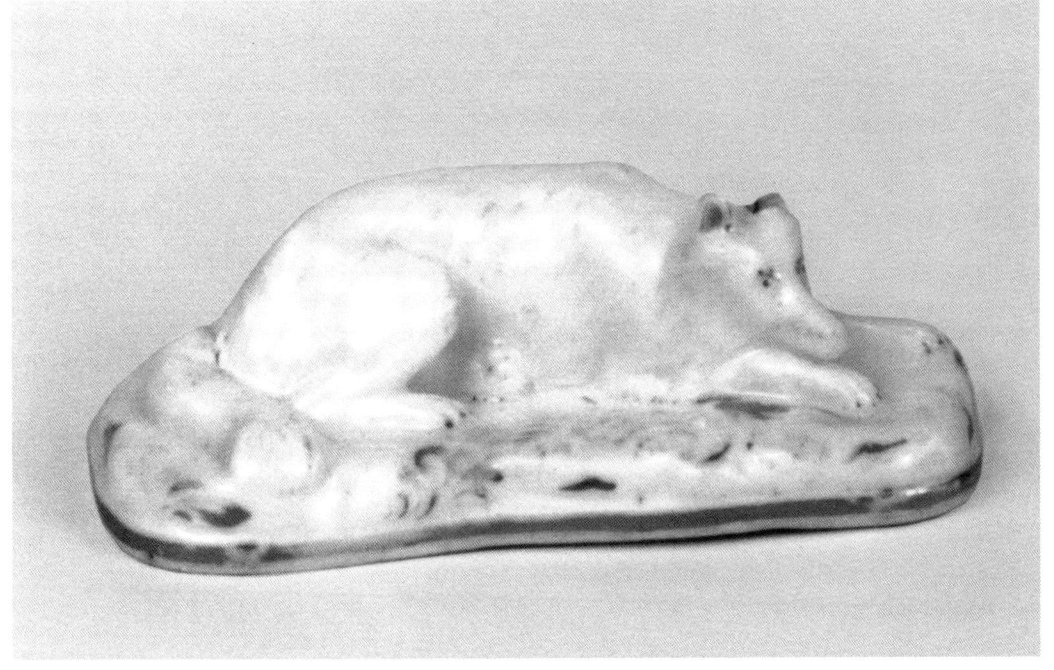

FIGURE 26. *Companion dog to that of Figure 25 in reverse. Note that the head is not raised.* Christie's

NEWFOUNDLANDS

As the name suggests, the breed came to this country from Newfoundland. There it was used as a draught animal. Teams consisting of three, four or five dogs were employed to drag sledges across the ice, often with loads of several hundred weight. They would travel without a driver to their destination, and on arrival were unloaded, whereupon they would return home with the empty sledge. It was only then that they were fed, often inadequately at that.

The Newfoundland acquired a great reputation for saving sailors – sometimes the whole ship's company – and others from drowning. It was often employed on board ship, both naval and merchant vessels, where it proved a keen retriever of property and personnel. It frequently became the ship's mascot.

It was but a short step from employment as a ship's dog to use as a working dog or pet. Because the Newfoundland had a great aptitude for retrieving it could be trained to perform all the duties of a gun dog. At the beginning of the nineteenth century it was the second most popular dog. In 1803 in a musical afterpiece at Drury Lane Theatre entitled 'The Caravan', a Newfoundland called Carlo created a sensation by plunging each night into water, with an audible splash, to rescue a child, which feat was received by the audience with rapturous applause.

In her memoirs Elizabeth Grant writes of the spring of 1803:

> Amongst other indulgences this spring I was taken twice to the play and once to Sadler's Wells with William. The first play was 'The Caravan'. John Kemble acted in it; the lover, and a very lugubrious one he seemed to be. The actor that delighted me was a dog, a real Newfoundland trained to leap into a cataract and bring dripping out of the water, *real* water, a doll representing a child which had spoken in the scene a few minutes before, and had then appeared to be dropped by a lady in distress while flying across a plank up at the top of the stage, the only bridge across the torrent. They could not persuade me [she was then six years old] the doll was not the real child: I thought it dead drowned, and cried and sobbed so violently I was hardly to be pacified – not till all the audience had been attracted by the noise.[124]

Another instance of the use of a Newfoundland dog on the stage is recorded in a letter of Prince Pückler-Muskau:

> But back to the play. It concluded with a melodrama, in which a large Newfoundland dog really acted admirably; he defended a banner for a long time, pursued the enemy and afterwards came on the stage wounded, lame and bleeding and died in the most masterly manner, with a last wag of the tail that was really full of genius. You would have sworn that the good beast knew at least as well as any of his human companions what he was about.[125]

The use of a Newfoundland dog on the stage did not stop in 1826. Such a dog appeared again on 18 October 1841 at the Theatre Royal, Worthing. For a Mr. H. Smith, of the Theatre Royal, Adelphi, played there with his Newfoundland dog Bruin in 'The Forest of Bondy, or The Dog of Montargis', an illustration of the animal appearing prominently on the playbill. The plot of the piece, and in particular the part played by

Bruin, is described in the playbill as follows:

> This truly interesting and affecting piece is founded on a well-known Historical fact and portrays the assassination of Capt Aubri, an Officer in the French Service in the Forest of Bondy, which Murder is brought to light by the sagacity of a Dog, that attended his master at the time; that not only makes known his death, but actually saves the life of an innocent person falsely accused as the perpetrator, and about to be led to Execution, by discovering the real Murderer.

H. Smith was engaged to appear at the Theatre Royal, Worthing for four nights running, and on 22 October 1841 he took part with his Newfoundland dog in 'The Dog of the Wreck'. The part played by Bruin is set out in the playbill as follows:

> **The Dog discovered watching the Hut Built by Morton** who with his wife and child have been shipwrecked on the Island.
> ARRIVAL OF THE BLOOD RED CHIEF WITH HIS TRIBE
> The chief becomes enamoured of the wife of the Captain on whose destruction he relies – At this junction an English ship is seen upon the Coast.
> A SIGNAL IS CONVEYED BY THE DOG TO THE SHIP
> The sailors land, and are hospitably entertained – a storm prevents them from embarking – they resolve to spend the night in Morton's Hut – Pattipaw [Smith] offers the Poisoned Liquor to the Captain – the Dog dashes the cup from his lips. Morton [Mr. Harris] determines to watch the movements of the Chief but overcome with fatigue falls asleep – the wily savage again attempts his life, but is a third time defeated by the sagacious dog – Morton's wife and son are carried off by the savages.
> *Broad Sword Combat* between Mr. H. SMITH and Mr. HARRIS. Morton is overcome, but cuts the cord which confines the Dog – FLIGHT OF PATTIPAW PURSUED BY THE DOG – The Indians bear the Wife and Child to a frightful ravine – Mrs. Morton still refuses the proffered love of the Chief. She is tied to a stake, the torch is lighted – *The affectionate dog rescues his mistress from the flames and the child from the fangs of a serpent.*
> A Combat between Miss Winter and Mr. H. Smith – The Indian is about to stab the Lady in the heart when the Dog enters and seizes him by the arm. The Piece concludes with a general skirmish between the British Sailors and the Savage
> *Deadly encounter with the Dog and Pattipaw*
> DEATH STRUGGLE WITH THE CHIEF – THE FAITHFUL DOG TRIUMPHANT.

Byron had a pet Newfoundland called Boatswain on whose death he erected a monument inscribing on the tomb an epitaph which concluded with the words: 'The poor dog! In life the firmest friend, The first to welcome, foremost to defend; whose honest heart is still his master's own; who labours, fights, lives, breathes for him alone'.

On 6 April 1903 as a result of a fight in London's Hyde Park between their respective Newfoundland dogs, Lt.-Col. Montgomery and Capt. MacNamara, R.N., fought a duel resulting in fatal consequences to the former and injury to the latter.

In view of the immense popularity of the Newfoundland at the beginning of the nineteenth century it is surprising not to find it prolifically represented in porcelain during the period with which we are concerned. However, a model was produced by the Grainger Lee factory (Figure 27). It was in a standing position on a mound base with its tongue hanging out, 4¾in. high. Another version, 6in. long and also standing, was turned out at Derby. Sometimes this version can be found with a small boy or small girl riding on the dog, in which event it is presumably identifiable with the John Whitaker models 'Boy and dog' and 'Girl and dog'. A fine pair, standing on flat oval bases, were exhibited at the Chelsea Antiques Fair of March 1998. The factory mark in red together with the number '31' also in red appeared under each base. An example of the dog standing by itself on an oval base with the Bloor Derby mark is also known.[126]

This particular model would seem to be based on the engraving by Bewick, which in turn was based on a drawing of:

> A very fine [animal] of Eslington, in the County of Northumberland. Its dimensions were as follows: – From its nose to the end of its tail, it measures six feet two inches; the length of its tail, one foot ten inches; from one fore foot right over its shoulders to the other, five feet seven inches; round its head over its ears, two feet; round the upper part of its fore leg nine inches and a half. It was web-footed [!], could swim extremely fast, dive with great ease, and bring up anything from the bottom of the water. It was naturally fond of fish; and ate raw trouts, or otherwise small fish out of the nets.

The Minton factory produced a fine model of a Newfoundland (Colour Plate 210). The same dog appears in the factory drawing book (No 21), but whereas in the drawing book it is free-standing without support, in the case of the animal actually produced it has a tree support and an elaborate base. It is to be noted that this particular model is not, like the Derby Newfoundland, based on the engraving by Thomas Bewick, but (like the Grainger Lee & Co. Newfoundland) on that by Philip Reinagle R.A. appearing in *The Sportsman's Cabinet*. Presumably, there was a reverse model in the form of a bitch. Sometimes the model is ridden by a small boy with a sword in his hand to represent war (illustration No 25 in the factory drawing book)[127] or by a girl with a crook to symbolise peace (illustration No 26).

The origin of the pair of Newfoundlands with black and ochre patches and red tongues illustrated in Colour Plate 211 is something of a mystery. The interesting feature is that one of the pair is, in its modelling, a replica of the Minton animal of Colour Plate 210, and the other is simply the companion in

Figure 27. *Grainger Lee Newfoundland with brown markings, standing on a mound base, its tongue hanging from its mouth. 4¾in. high. Marked in red script 'Grainger Lee & Co'. c.1820–37.*

Sotheby's

COLOUR PLATE 210. *Minton white and gilt Newfoundland with tongue hanging out, standing beside a tree support on a high rocky mound base. 3⅝in. high. c.1831–40.*

COLOUR PLATE 211. *Pair of Staffordshire Newfoundlands, each with a red tongue hanging out, decorated in black and ochre, standing with trunk support on a high rocky mound base. 3½in. high. c.1835–50.*

reverse.[128] They are not, however, from the Minton factory. They lack the Minton quality, both as regards the porcelain and the decoration, and each of the bases, instead of being closed-in with a centrally located hole, is left entirely open. Presumably, some unknown Staffordshire factory simply copied the Minton version.

COLOUR PLATE 212. *Pair of Staffordshire Newfoundlands, each lying recumbent with a child clambering about its neck on an elaborately scrolled base. 4½in. long. c.1835–50.* John Read Antiques

Another pair of Staffordshire Newfoundlands are shown in Colour Plate 212. In each case, a child is climbing over the dog's neck. Other Staffordshire Newfoundlands are also recorded, usually with the tongue hanging out. An interesting example dressed as a foxhunter with a child riding it appeared in Christie's South Kensington sale (26 October 2000, Lot 341).

The Parian group consisting of a small boy about to mount a Newfoundland, as shown in Colour Plate 213, is probably from the Samuel Alcock factory. Though unmarked, the texture and colour of the Parian would appear to be indistinguishable from those of a marked Samuel Alcock group of a shepherdess and sheep.[129] The group of Colour Plate 213 was doubtless based on an engraving. The Samuel Alcock factory also modelled a Newfoundland to accompany a human figure, impressed '231'.

Finally, what seems to be a Newfoundland can be seen in each of the two Robinson and Leadbeater Parian groups of terriers and Newfoundlands illustrated in Figure 31 (page 147).

COLOUR PLATE 213. *Parian group consisting of a small boy wearing a Tam o' Shanter hat, a dress and trousers, about to mount a Newfoundland standing with head turned back and tail stretched out, the tip upturned, standing on a circular base, lightly scrolled around the edges. 6in. high. Probably from the Samuel Alcock factory. c.1850–60.*

COLOUR PLATE 214. *Samuel Alcock saluki or Persian greyhound with grey markings seated on a yellow rocky mound base. 3½in. high. Impressed '311'. c.1840–50. This model is impressed with the same number as that appearing under the poodle in Colour Plate 67. As two different models could not carry the same number, the factory clearly made a mistake, but in the absence of further examples it is impossible to say which model is correctly numbered.*

SALUKIS/PERSIAN GREYHOUNDS

The saluki is an Arab dog, whose origin goes back thousands of years, appearing in Egyptian carvings of about 6000 to 5000 B.C. Throughout the nineteenth century it was used in hunting the gazelle, often in conjunction with the hawk. Salukis can gallop for miles over the sands of Arabia and over rough ground that would break every bone in an English greyhound. Whereas gazelles are credited with speeds of between 45 and 52 mph, Salukis reach between 37 and 40mph. Nevertheless, although slower than the gazelle, this handicap was compensated for in the following manner. The dogs would separate a gazelle from the bewildered herd and then by their various manoeuvres would so terrorise the animal that it eventually tired. They would then draw level with it and strike. Sometimes they would chase a gazelle in a circle, eventually killing it at the point where the chase began. Often the Saluki was used in conjunction with a hawk. On the release of the latter, the saluki was slipped from its leash to pursue the game by following the flight of the hawk. When the latter 'stooped' on the gazelle, the saluki was expected to come up and hold the creature until the riders arrived for the kill.

In Persia the saluki was known as the Persian greyhound. An interesting print exists of a Persian greyhound bitch, Zillah, after the painting by C. Hamilton dated 1837. A note on the back states that the animal was 'the property of Mr. George Lock, Kentish Town, bred in the Zoological Gardens, Regent's Park, 1835. She is the only thoroughbred bitch at present in this country'.[130] It was not until 1897 that the saluki was properly introduced into this country, but it was not registered as a breed by the Kennel Club until 1922. Salukis rarely feature in porcelain. However, three factories at

Colour Plate 215. *Minton Persian greyhound in Parian seated on a high rocky base. 7in. high. Model No 119 in the factory drawing book. c.1850–70.*

least did make them, namely Samuel Alcock (Colour Plate 214), Minton (Colour Plate 215) and Madeley (Colour Plates 216 and 217).

The Minton saluki or Persian greyhound, which is really a larger version of the Samuel Alcock model, is numbered 119 in the factory drawing book. The example illustrated is in Parian and replaced a setter in biscuit, which previously appeared in the list under that number. The model is often paired with No 120 (Colour Plate 6), an Italian greyhound, although the real dogs they represent are quite dissimilar in size.

The saluki illustrated in Colour Plate 216 comes from the Madeley factory. It has grey

markings and lies recumbent on a rocky base, 5in. long, splashed with turquoise and edged with a continuous apple green line. There is no gilding. Like Rockingham, Derby and early Minton animals, the underneath of the base is closed in save for a centrally located hole. The example is seen side by side with a Madeley goat whose distinctive turquoise markings help to identify the dog with the Madeley factory. A larger version of the saluki of Colour Plate 216 is illustrated in Colour Plate 217. The dog is brown and lies on the same rocky base, albeit 6in. long, but this time the base is splashed with gilding, not turquoise.

COLOUR PLATE 216.
Madeley saluki with grey markings lying recumbent on a rocky mound base splashed with turquoise decoration and edged with a continuous apple green line. 5in. long. c.1830. Seen with a Madeley goat.

COLOUR PLATE 217.
Larger version of the dog of Colour Plate 216. 6in. long. c.1830
Andrew Dando Antiques

TERRIERS

Terriers, which were in our period an important breed in this country, were used to kill rats and dig out foxes and badgers. Dr. Caius, writing in the sixteenth century, says of them:

> Another sorte there is which hunteth the fox and the badger or greye only, whom we call terriers; they creep into the ground, and by that means make afrayde, nyppe and bite the fox and the badger in such sorte that they eyther teare them in pieces with theyr teeth, beying in bosome of the earth, or else hoyl and pull them per force out of their lurking angles, dark dungeons and close caves.

Terriers often took part in rat-killing contests, as is vividly recounted by Prince Pückler-Muskau, when he describes the exploits of a terrier called Billy who not only killed rats, but fought with badgers.

> In a suburb, a good German mile from my lodging [in London], we entered a sort of barn; dirty, with no other ceiling than the rough roof, through which the moon peeped here and there. In the middle was a boarded place, about twelve feet square, surrounded by a strong wooden breastwork; round this was a gallery filled with the lowest vulgar and with perilous-looking faces of both sexes. A ladder led up to a higher gallery, for the patrician part of the spectators, which was let out at three shillings a seat. There was a strange contrast between the 'local' [place] and a crystal lustre hanging from one of the balks of the roof, lighted with thick wax candles; as well as between the 'fashionables' and the populace among whom they were scattered, who – the latter I mean – were continually offering and taking bets of from twenty to fifty pounds. The subject of these was a fine terrier, the illustrious Billy, who pledged himself to the public to kill a hundred rats in ten minutes. As yet the arena was empty, and there was an anxious, fearful pause; while in the lower gallery pots of beer circulated from mouth to mouth, and tobacco-smoke ascended in dense clouds. At length appeared a strong man, bearing a sack looking like a sack of potatoes, but in fact containing the hundred live rats. These he set at liberty in one moment by untying the knot, scattered them about the place, and rapidly made his retreat into a corner. At a given signal Billy rushed in, and set about his murderous work with incredible fury. As soon as a rat lay lifeless, Billy's faithful esquire picked him up and put him in the sack; among those some might be only senseless, or perhaps there might be some old practitioners who feigned themselves dead at the first bite. However, be that as it may, Billy won in nine minutes and a quarter, according to all the watches; in which time a hundred dead, or apparently dead, rats were replaced in their old quarters – the sack. This was the first act. In the second, the heroic Billy (who was greeted with the continual shouts of an enraptured audience), fought with a badger. Each of the combatants had a second, who held him by the tail. Only one bite or gripe was allowed; then they were separated, and immediately let loose again. Billy had always the best of it, and the poor badger's ears streamed with blood. In this combat, too, Billy was bound to seize the badger fast in a certain number of minutes – I don't recollect how many. This he accomplished in brilliant style, but retired at last greatly exhausted.[131]

A description of a less formal rat catching exercise is described by a daughter of the Victorian painter W. Frith:

COLOUR PLATE 218. *Rockingham terrier decorated in fawn lying recumbent on a maroon rectangular base with pinched-in sections. 3¼in. long. Incised 'No 87'. Cl. 2. Impressed mark. 1826–30.*

> Mr. Pearce came to town [about 1868 when the writer would have been about twenty] to perform the ceremony when my sister was married, and the moment the bridal pair had departed he turned to me. 'Off with that finery; I am going to see Bill George [a celebrated dog fancier with 'the most remarkable collection of dogs I ever saw']. In less than five seconds I was in my walking dress, and off we started, and had a lovely time hearing about all the dogs, and finally seeing a splendid fox-terrier turned into a species of pit, where he disposed of about a dozen rats in less time that it takes to tell of it.[132]

The Rockingham factory was responsible for three terrier models (Nos 87, 88 and 89). Model No 87 is illustrated in Colour Plates 218 and 219. Model No 88, illustrated in

COLOUR PLATE 219. *Two Rockingham white and gilt terriers, each lying recumbent on a rectangular base with pinched-in sections. 3¼in. long. Incised 'No 87'. Impressed mark. 1826–30.*

Figure 28, would appear to be the standing version of No 87. Model No 89 is shown in Colour Plate 220 and Figures 29 and 30.

The example of No 89 shown in Figure 30 is interesting for the fact that, in contrast to the group in Colour Plate 220 and Figure 29, the rat is in a cage. The cage was made as a separate item quite independent of the animal group, and was intended to be placed on the base over the rat. Its remarkable preservation must be attributed to the fact that, together with the dog and the rat, it was protected by a glass dome that covered the entire group.

Whether a cage was invariably made to accompany this model is problematic. So far, only three examples of model No 89 have come to light, and in only one instance has a cage been found. A simple and obvious explanation is, of course, that the cage invariably accompanied the group, but because it was both fragile and separate, it was normally lost or destroyed. But is this necessarily the solution? It is to be noted that in the case of the two examples of No 89 illustrated in Colour Plate 220 and Figure 29, the rat looks away from the dog, whilst in the case of the other specimen the rat turned towards the dog.

FIGURE 28. *Rockingham terrier with cropped ears standing with curled upright tail on a mound base, in biscuit. 3in. high. Incised 'No 88'. Impressed mark. 1826–30.* Phillips

FIGURE 29. *Rockingham terrier looking at a rat on a rectangular mound base, in biscuit. 5in. long. Incised 'No 89'. Impressed mark. 1826–30. Compare the white and gilt example of Colour Plate 220.*

FIGURE 30. *Rockingham terrier looking at a rat in a cage, standing on a rectangular mound base, in biscuit. 5in. long. Incised 'No 89'. Impressed mark. 1826–30. The cage is a separate entity. Compare Figure 29 and Colour Plate 220.* Christie's

Possibly no significance is to be attached to the difference of position – it could have depended on the whim of the repairer. But an alternative explanation could be that the factory found it unsatisfactory producing the cage and decided to discontinue it as a feature.[133] However, it would have been somewhat unnatural to have left the rat facing the dog – a rat seeing the dog would have fled – and accordingly the factory presented

COLOUR PLATE 220. *Rockingham white and gilt terrier looking at a rat on a rectangular mound base. 5in. long. Model No 89, but unnumbered. Cl. 1. 1826–30. For biscuit examples see Figures 29 and 30.*

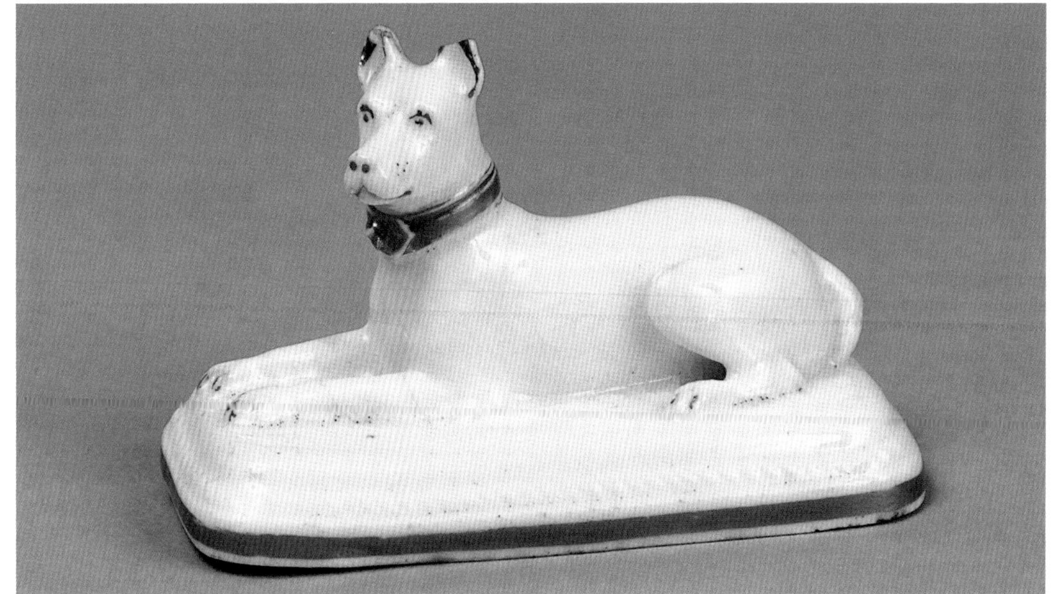

Colour Plate 221. *Grainger Lee white and gilt terrier lying recumbent on a base edged with a continuous rope moulding. 3¼in. long. Impressed 'GRAINGER LEE & CO WORCESTER'. 1820–37.*

a more normal scenario by turning the rat round to indicate that it had not seen the dog and was not in the process of escaping. If this theory is right, models with the rat turned away from the dog never had a cage.

The Grainger Lee factory also produced terriers. A model lying recumbent can be seen in Colour Plate 221. This particular model does not appear in the factory's pattern book. However, the following entry appears in one of the factory's note books:[134]

	Gilt	Coloured proper	Plain
Tirrier [*sic*] lying	1/8	2/-	1/4

Presumably, this description refers to the model of Colour Plate 221. However, the

Colour Plate 222. *Grainger Lee white and gilt terrier with front leg raised, sniffing a rat and standing unsupported on a flat rectangular-shaped base made to simulate floor boards, elaborately gilded at the edges and with canted corners. 5in. long. Mark: 'GRAINGER LEE & CO WORCESTER', lightly impressed. 1820–37.*

FIGURE 31. *Pair of Robinson and Leadbeater terrier puppy and Newfoundland groups in Parian entitled 'Impudence' and 'Retribution' respectively. 11in. long. Design registered 2 July 1872.* Godden of Worthing Ltd.

COLOUR PLATE 223. *Staffordshire terrier with black patches standing on a green rectangular base. 1⅞in. long. c.1830–50.*
Christie's South Kensington

pattern book does include a terrier looking at a rat in a cage, somewhat similar to the Rockingham group 'No 89'. A porcelain example of this model has now come to light, and is shown in Colour Plate 222. The wire cage seen in the factory pattern book has long ago been lost. The dog – and it is a dog, not a bitch – stands on a base made to look like floorboards, rectangular in shape, with canted corners. The base, which is elaborately gilded at the edges, is 5in. long. (How a real rat was introduced into a wire cage is described in Smith.)

A particularly attractive terrier from somewhere in Staffordshire is illustrated in Colour Plate 223. See also the terrier and Newfoundland groups of Figure 31 (p.147).

WOLF DOGS/DOG OF ALCIBIADES

The Minton factory produced a dog illustrated in its drawing book (No 227) which is there described as a 'wolf dog'. Unfortunately, it is a replica of the 'Dog of Alcibiades', and this has inevitably given rise to confusion.

That there was such an animal as a wolf dog is substantiated by a passage from *The Gardens and Menagerie of the Zoological Society Delineated* which reads as follows:[135]

> Although regarded by Buffon, in common with the shepherd's dog, as an example of the species in the very lowest stage of cultivation, but one degree removed from a state of nature, the present variety is in fact one of the most intellectual of all the races of Dogs. By continued intercourse with man these valuable dogs have become more highly improved, in all that constitutes moral superiority, than almost any other breed; the Newfoundland Dog, the Esquimaux, and the Spaniel alone evincing an equal share of docility, fidelity and intelligence.
>
> According to Buffon, the breed in question are denominated Wolf Dogs, 'because they resemble the Wolf in ears and length of hair'. Their ears, it is true, are of small size, and frequently erect; but they have a strong tendency to become pendulous, as is actually the case in the Society's specimens, and thereby approach more closely to the spaniels. Their hair too is long and straight, but by no means like that of the Wolf; and we can hardly conceive a greater contrast in physiognomy and general appearance than is presented by the two animals. Others again have derived their name from the services which they render to the shepherd in protecting his flock from the nightly marauder; but though strong-built and muscular both in body and limb, they seem too gentle in their disposition to be peculiarly adapted for pulling down so powerful and ferocious an animal as a wolf.

Wolf dogs were kept in the Regent's Park Zoo in London. A Hungarian wolf dog was first exhibited there in 1828 and an Italian wolf dog in 1827 or 1828.[136] But independent evidence of the existence of wolf dogs can be found in a passage from the reminiscences of Mary Boyle:[137]

> In the backyard of the Rectory [Wigan, Lancashire, the home of Mary Boyle's uncle] a magnificent wolf-dog lived in the kennel, the object of universal terror among the servants and gardeners. But I believed in and trusted dogs, and my firm conviction was that Lupus was misunderstood. I bribed the servants to let me feed him, which I did first at a respectful distance, advancing nearer and nearer each day as I presented him with his dinner. At length I deemed him tamed, and, not without slight trepidation, I approached, let slip his collar, and opened the garden gate. Never shall I forget the consternation the apparition of girl and dog caused in my aunt's little sitting-room which opened on the lawn. She was talking to my mother in this sanctum when she saw Lupus bounding over the grass and standing on the threshold of her boudoir. With a loud cry the Rector's wife jumped upon the chair, gathering her skirts around her, and summoning her juvenile protectress to call off the dog. But Lupus did no harm; he was only elated by his new-born freedom, and he became from that day the constant companion of the daily walks I took with my youngest brother and our nurse.

But what did wolf dogs really look like?

It would seem that the wolf dogs in the zoo were the equivalent of, or closely related to, the Irish wolfhound, an animal of enormous size and capable of overpowering a mastiff.[138] However, it was essentially of a passive and gentle disposition. It became extinct about 1840, but was reconstructed by Captain Graham in the 1880s. The Irish wolfhound was shaped rather like a greyhound but stouter. But if the Irish wolfhound was essentially of a passive and gentle disposition, how can this characteristic be reconciled with the assessment of its disposition made by Buffon and, in the case of the animal described by Mary Boyle, with the effect it had on those having dealings with it? The answer would seem to be that the Irish wolfhound could be a most ferocious and formidable animal, presenting a terrifying appearance, with all the physical power to back it up, and if treated simply as a guard dog without any attempt to soften its demeanour; it was indeed an unattractive animal. However, if handled kindly and its trust won over, it became a tranquil and amicable companion.

Although there were wolf dogs in existence from about 1818 to 1840, they do not seem to have corresponded in appearance with the dog illustrated in the Minton drawing book and there described as a 'wolf dog'. In truth that dog represented the Dog of Alcibiades discussed below. Did the Minton factory intend to produce a wolf dog to which they inaccurately gave the form of the Dog of Alcibiades, or did they mean to turn out a porcelain model of the Dog of Alcibiades, which, instead of calling it by its right name, they chose to entitle inaccurately a wolf dog? It is impossible to be certain, but on the balance of probability I consider the latter alternative to be the more likely.

The Dog of Alcibiades is a marble statue (twice life size) of a Molossian dog, ancestor of the modern mastiff. It is Roman, belonging to the second century A.D., after a lost Greek original, probably executed in bronze. It was acquired in Rome between 1748 and 1756 by an Englishman named Jennings. The previous owner was the sculptor Bartolomeo Cavaceppi (?1716–99) who was the foremost restorer of his day and who, before selling it to Jennings, had restored the statue – the muzzle, the left foreleg, small patches on the body and all four sides of the plinth are replacements, whilst the tip of the tail is missing. Jennings brought the dog back to England and received the nickname 'Dog Jennings'. He called the dog Dog of Alcibiades, a reference to the dog once owned by the Greek politician Alcibiades. According to Plutarch, Alcibiades cut off his dog's tail. When the citizens of Athens expressed indignation at Alcibiades' conduct, he replied that he 'wished the Athenians to talk about this, that they might not say something worse of me'.

Owing to his debts, largely incurred by his passion for horseracing, Jennings had to sell the statue, which in 1778 at Christie's made £1,000 guineas. The purchaser was Charles Duncombe of Duncombe Park in Yorkshire.[139] Walpole considered the Molossian among the five principal statues of animals from antiquity. No other animal from antiquity has survived in so many Roman copies. Six are known to exist.

What was the intended breed of the pair of Samuel Alcock dogs shown in Colour Plate 224 poses considerable difficulty. They are similar to the Dog of Alcibiades, but they do not correspond exactly. They sit with cropped ears, thick fur and ferocious expression, each on a high mound base, their open menacing mouths suggesting their suitability for inclusion in the schedule to the Dangerous Dogs Act. Were they intended to represent wolf dogs?

The base of one of the dogs is yellow, the other green. The decoration of both dogs

COLOUR PLATE 224. *Pair of Samuel Alcock wolf dogs, each with cropped ears, thick fur and ferocious expression, seated on a high rocky mound base, yellow in one case, green in the other. 4in. high. Impressed '253'. c.1840–50.*

COLOUR PLATE 225. *White-glazed model of the Dog of Alcibiades from the King Street factory, Derby. 5½in. high. Sampson Hancock mark in blue. Later nineteenth century.*

is the same, so that although the bases are differently coloured, the animals must have continued together from the time they left the factory, or at least from the time they were sold by the retailer to the ultimate purchaser. Perhaps the purchaser preferred the variation in colours and specifically demanded a pair with different coloured bases. But in any event, it is unlikely in the extreme that they were subsequently matched.

One of the pair is impressed under the base '2 3', the other with what looks like '253'. In the latter case the '5' and '3' are quite distinct, but the '2' is barely discernible. As regards the other animal there is a considerable gap between the '2' and '3' (both of which figures are legible without difficulty) suggesting that the factory omitted to impress the further number '5'.

The Dog of Alcibiades was reproduced in various materials, including Coade stone together with a companion in reverse to make a pair. An undoubted porcelain version of the Dog of Alcibiades was made by the King Street factory at Derby. An example glazed white is shown in Colour Plate 225. It carries the factory mark in blue.

COLOUR PLATE 226. *White-glazed model of a Pekingese in a begging position from the King Street factory, Derby. 2¾in. high. Sampson Hancock mark in blue. Later nineteenth century.*

MISCELLANEOUS DOGS

Sandon has shown from examination of the Royal Worcester records that in 1873 the factory modelled a Skye terrier (in two sizes, item 374 in the factory list), in 1874 a Spitz dog (item 443) and a St. Bernard (item 444), and in 1876 a dachshund (item 550). It should also be mentioned that in 1862 the factory modelled a group of 'dogs and rat' (item 25) and a group of 'dog and pheasant'.

The King Street factory, Derby, produced a Pekingese (Colour Plate 226) and a dachshund (Colour Plate 227).

DOG COLLARS

Before leaving the discussion of porcelain dogs of the nineteenth century a brief reference should be made to certain types of collars some of them are shown wearing, notably shepherd's dogs and poodles.

Specially designed collars were used on the Continent to protect shepherd's dogs. Examples from the sixteenth century made in Germany of iron, with outward spikes to safeguard the dog's neck against wolves and bears, are to be seen in The Dog Collar Museum, Leeds Castle, Maidstone, Kent. The dog that accompanies the shepherd of Colour Plate 206 has a protective collar, from which it can be inferred that the model was based on a Continental original.

Dog collars appear in paintings. A graphic illustration of a Continental dog with a spiked collar can be seen in 'A Huntsman Cutting up a Dead Deer with two Deerhounds',[140] by Jan Baptist Weenix (1621–?60/1). Presumably, in this instance the spiked collar was to protect the dog from any retaliation on the part of the stag when at bay. In contrast, pet dogs on the Continent often appear in paintings with collars fitted with a

COLOUR PLATE 227. *White-glazed model of a dachshund from the King Street factory, Derby. 4½in. long. Sampson Hancock mark in blue. Later nineteenth century.*

COLOUR PLATE 228. *Two Staffordshire seated musicians, each accompanied by his dog seated at his feet. 4½in. and 4¾in. high respectively. c.1840–50. The dog that accompanies the larger piper would appear to be a King Charles spaniel, but the breed of the dog on the left defies identification.*

series of round metal balls, for example, the pet dog with such a collar in the mid-1540s painting by Titian of 'The Vendramin Family'.[141] Henry VIII's dogs, including his greyhounds which he used for hunting, wore collars of velvet. In the eighteenth century, royalty preferred silver, but Queen Victoria reverted to velvet for her lap-dogs.

It would seem that the collars appearing on the Derby pug dogs shown in Colour Plate 24 and the corresponding Rockingham pug dogs of Colour Plate 21 are fitted with balls rather than studs. Presumably this was because they were based on Continental models.

Some porcelain dogs do not normally have a collar at all, but when they do have one, and are not left in the biscuit, such a collar is generally gilded and often has a padlock (for example Colour Plate 20).

The History and Output of the Factories

ROCKINGHAM

The finest porcelain animals to be produced in this country in the nineteenth century were probably those made at the Rockingham factory, which was located at Swinton, near Rotherham, Yorkshire. The factory was, during its short life as a porcelain producer, under the patronage of Earl Fitzwilliam and depended upon him for financial support, taking its name from the Earl's relative the Marquess of Rockingham. In 1806 the factory, which had produced earthenware from about the middle of the eighteenth century, came under the ownership of the Brameld family. However, by 1826, the business had become insolvent and it was only saved from extinction by the timely financial assistance of Earl Fitzwilliam. The Brameld brothers – Thomas, George and John Wager – had persuaded him that they were capable of manufacturing porcelain, and that, given the requisite financial backing, they could equal, not to say surpass, in quality the products of all contemporary factories. In the event, they were largely successful in this ambition, turning out, *inter alia*, the famous Royal Service for William IV. However, their financial management was not on a par with their artistic attainments, and in 1842 the Earl's successor, despairing of the Bramelds ever getting the factory to pay its way, withdrew all further support and the production of this outstanding nineteenth century factory came to an end.

The output of the Rockingham factory was varied in the extreme comprising ornamental ware, useful ware and figures, and included some beautifully modelled dogs, perhaps the finest dogs to be produced in nineteenth century English porcelain. Most Rockingham dogs are marked, sometimes with the impressed words under the base 'Rockingham Works/Brameld', with or without an impressed Griffin,[1] at other times simply with the letters 'Cl'[2] written (normally in script) in red, gold, mauve, or black followed by a similarly written '1' in the case of white and gilt examples, and '2' in the case of gilt and enamelled specimens.[3] Not infrequently, both types of mark appear together. Very rarely, variations of the impressed mark are found, e.g. the words 'Rockingham Works' appear alone or the single word 'Brameld', and in certain instances, almost certainly early models (e.g. the pug bitch of Colour Plate 20), in place of the impressed mark there is to be seen the printed Red Griffin mark consisting of the Griffin and the words in two rows underneath 'Rockingham Works/Brameld' all printed in red.

Rockingham dogs were normally incised with their model number, preceded by the letters 'No'. Moreover, this number, even in the absence of a factory mark, is enough to identify the animal with the factory. It is not possible to say for certain that the numbers employed have any chronological significance. In other words, the numbers may not indicate the order in which the relevant models were brought into existence. There is no proof that the lower numbers antedated the higher.[4] Moreover, some dog models, e.g. the pugs of Colour Plate 20, seem never to have been distinguished by a number. Presumably, these pugs were early models discontinued before the numbering system was put into operation, and replaced by the pug models of Colour Plate 21, which are both incised 'No 76'.

Incised model numbers are not found on contemporary Derby models. The only incised numbers appearing on the latter are '1', '2' or '3' without the prefix 'No' and these were intended to indicate size, a practice likewise, but less frequently adopted at Swinton.[5]

Rockingham dogs are recorded in biscuit (Colour Plate 167 and Figures 9, 22, 28, 29 and 30), but more frequently they are glazed. In the latter form they are either white and gilt or enamelled and gilt (compare Colour Plate 218 with Colour Plate 219). As in the case of the contemporary Derby models, their underneath is flat, unglazed and closed-in save for a small round hole centrally located (Figure 16). Dogs are usually modelled as individual pieces, but occasionally they form part of a group (Colour Plate 205; Figure 22).

A particular feature of Rockingham dogs (and for that matter Rockingham figures generally) is that they can be dated to within a comparatively short period, namely 1826 to about 1830. This last point is extremely important in the study of English nineteenth century porcelain animals, which are notoriously difficult to date with any precision. For, by being able to attribute the Rockingham models to a brief period of some four or five years, we have a comparative yardstick by which to date other porcelain animals produced by other factories.

The reason for supposing that Rockingham dogs were only made during the opening four to five years of the factory's life as a porcelain producer is based on the form of the mark used (where the mark is the full version and not merely a 'Cl' with the numbers '1' or '2'). As explained earlier, that mark consists of the impressed words 'Rockingham Works/Brameld' with or without an impressed griffin, or very rarely the printed mark in red. Not all examples were so marked, but where they were, the use of the early form of mark, which makes no reference to the factory's being 'Royal' or to its being 'Manufacturer to the King' (descriptions assumed as part of the mark after this order for the Royal Service had been received in 1830), would indicate that all Rockingham dogs are to be assigned to the period from 1826 to 1830 or slightly later.[6]

Set out below is a list of Rockingham models so far recorded.

MODEL NO	DESCRIPTION	HEIGHT	LENGTH	WIDTH	ILLUSTRATION
4	A shepherd and dog group '18th century version'	7¼in.			Colour Plate 206
	Later version	8½in.			Colour Plate 205
35	A boy standing on a pierced scroll base with a King Charles spaniel	5¾in.			Figure 10
58	A 'Continental' shepherd with a dog and sheep	7¾in.			Figure 22
71	A toy foxhound sitting	1⅛in.			Colour Plate 200
74	A toy foxhound sitting	1⅜in.			Colour Plate 200
75	Possibly a begging pug[7]	2¼in.			Colour Plate 23a
76	A pug dog seated				
	First size	2⅝in.			Colour Plate 21
	Second size	2⅛in.			Colour Plate 21
	A pug bitch seated	2⅝in.			Colour Plate 22a

MODEL NO	DESCRIPTION	HEIGHT	LENGTH	WIDTH	ILLUSTRATION
83	A springer spaniel running	2⅞in.	3¼in.		Colour Plate 122
84	A standing setter about to drink from a bowl	3¼in.	3¾in.		Colour Plate 167
85	Foxhound bitch standing	4¼in.	4⅝in.		Colour Plate 199
87	A recumbent terrier with head raised	2⅝in.	3¾in.	2⅜in.	Colour Plate 218 Colour Plate 219
88	A standing terrier	3in.			Figure 28
89	A standing terrier watching a rat, sometimes with a cage	3¼in.	5in.	2¼in.	Colour Plate 220 Figures 29 and 30
90	A recumbent mastiff with tongue hanging out	1⅝in.	4⅝in.	1¾in.	Colour Plate 197
91	A spaniel curled up (presumably there was a companion in reverse)	1⅛in.	2⅝in.	1⅝in.	Colour Plate 126b and Figure 9a
92	A pointer dog lying recumbent	2¼in.	3¾in.	2¼in.	Colour Plate 184
	A pointer bitch in reverse	2¼in.	3¾in.	2¼in.	Colour Plate 184
93	A Spanish pointer bitch trotting (presumably there was a reversecompanion dog)	2¼in.	4½in.		Figure 18
94	A setter lying recumbent with head raised	2in.	4¼in.	2¼in.	Colour Plates 126a, 165 and 166 and Figure 9b
	The above animal in reverse	2in.	4¼in.	2¼in.	
96	A toy seated setter	1¾in.			Colour Plate 168
97	A seated poodle	3in.			Colour Plate 43
101	A seated pointer dog looking upwards	2¾in./3in.			Colour Plate 185 and Figure 19
	A seated pointer bitch looking upwards (in reverse)	2¾in./3in.			Colour Plates 185 and 186b
121	A begging pug	2½in.			Colour Plate 23b
UNNUMBERED MODELS					
	A pug dog sitting on an oval base		2⅝in.		Colour Plate 20
	A pug bitch sitting on an oval base		2½in.		Colour Plate 20
	A greyhound lying with its head supported on its forepaws on a base moulded with leaves			4in.	
	Silhouette or half-back model group of a pair of greyhounds, the bitch standing, the dog lying recumbent		2 13/16in		Figure 1

DERBY (Nottingham Road)
The Derby factory came into existence about 1750. Its early history[8] is not altogether clear. It appears originally to have been owned by Andrew Planché, a silversmith by training. In January 1756 Planché was joined by William Duesbury, a china decorator, and John Heath, a banker, but shortly thereafter Planché left the partnership and disappeared from the scene altogether.[9] The management of the factory devolved on William Duesbury, albeit John Heath remained a partner until his bankruptcy in 1780. Thereafter William Duesbury continued sole owner until his death in 1786, when he was succeeded by his son, also called William. The latter died in 1796 or 1797, but prior to his demise, when his health was failing, he took into partnership one Michael Kean, a considerable artist in his own right. In 1798 Michael Kean married Duesbury's widow. Her eldest son, William Duesbury III, was then only eleven years old, and, of course, too young to assume control of the business. However, when he reached maturity he never really took any interest in the concern and eventually left the town of Derby.

In 1809 the business was advertised for sale and in 1810 or 1811 was sold to Robert Bloor, who agreed to pay, in addition to certain annuities to the family of the late proprietor, £5,000 in instalments. Robert Bloor had been employed as a clerk and salesman under Duesbury and Kean. In order to pay off the instalments he resorted to the highly dubious expedient of selling by auction various 'seconds' which had accumulated at the factory under his predecessors. He was responsible for some debasement in the standard of decoration, which had hitherto applied. In consequence, the business suffered a decline in reputation during the Bloor period of control. In 1828 Bloor became insane and the management of the business fell to James Thomason who discharged his duties both honestly and competently. In 1844 Thomas Clark, malster and corn factor, married Bloor's granddaughter and sole surviving descendant and 'took out a Statute of Lunacy'. He carried on the works until 1848 when they were finally closed down, and the whole plant was sold to Samuel Boyle of Fenlon.[10] Derby animals of the first half of the nineteenth century[11] are of high quality, falling only marginally short of the standard set by the Rockingham factory, and they include dogs.

Derby dogs, unlike their Rockingham counterparts, are never numbered, and rarely marked. (Certain marked examples are illustrated in Colour Plates 25, 44, 45b and 187). Some models were made in up to three different sizes, and the size is sometimes indicated by an incised '1' (the largest), '2' or '3', as the case may be. The bases, like those of Rockingham dogs, are closed-in save for a centrally located hole. Derby dogs were normally produced as individual models, but they were sometimes also included in a group.

A list of Derby dog models, so far recorded, is set out below.

Description	Height	Length	Illustration
Greyhounds			
Standing greyhound	2⅝in.		Colour Plate 1 and Figure 3
Pugs			
Pug seated on a scrolled base (made in pairs)			
Size 1	3¼/3in.		
Size 2	2⅝in.		Colour Plate 24
Size 3	2¼in.		Colour Plates 22b and 24

DESCRIPTION	HEIGHT	LENGTH	ILLUSTRATION
Pug seated on a rectangular base (made in pairs)	3¼in.		Colour Plate 25
Pug seated on a rectangular base supported on four ball feet	3¼in.		
Pug begging	3½/2¼in.		
Pug seated on a rectangular base continued from eighteenth century	3½		
Poodles			
Pair of poodles, the dog scratching, the bitch with a more elegant pose, recumbent on an elaborately scrolled base		4/4½in.	Colour Plates 44 and 45
Toy poodle begging	1¼in.		Colour Plate 50a
Spaniel			
Spaniel curled up		3⅜in.	Colour Plate 127
Pointers and Setters			
Seated pointer looking upwards (both dog and bitch)	2½in.		Colour Plate 186a
Recumbent pointer and setter, pair		5in.	Colour Plates 169, 170 and 188
Trotting pointer and setter, pair		6½in.	Figure 17
Standing pointer with tree support	2⅜in.		Colour Plate 187
Newfoundlands			
Standing Newfoundland as an independent model		6in.	
Standing Newfoundland ridden by a boy or a girl		6in.	
Shepherd's Dogs	2½in.		Figure 23

DERBY (King Street)
In 1848 the great Derby factory in the Nottingham Road closed. However, a year later William Locker, who had been the last manager there, with the aid of five fellow employees from the old works, including Sampson Hancock (who alone of them had not been apprenticed there), founded a new manufactory in King Street trading under the name of the 'Old Crown China Works'. In 1859 Locker died. He was succeeded by Stevenson, a draper, when the billheads bore the title 'Stevenson & Co.'. However, according to Haslem[12] the firm traded as 'Stevenson and Hancock'. In 1866 Stevenson died, after which the firm was taken over by Sampson Hancock as sole proprietor and traded as 'Sampson Hancock & Co.'. This name continued in use after the death of Sampson Hancock in 1895. The factory's usual mark is in the form of the old Nottingham Road mark – a crown over dots, batons and a 'D' – but with the addition of the letter 'S' on one side and the letter 'H' on the other. According to Haslem[13] the letters stood

initially for 'Stevenson and Hancock' and later for 'Sampson Hancock'. The mark was used from about 1863 onwards. The factory remained as a small concern throughout its existence, but it survived until 1935, when it was taken over by the present Royal Crown Derby Porcelain Company Ltd. The latter company was founded in 1876 and occupied premises in Osmanton Road, about one mile from King Street and the Nottingham Road site. It was originally known as the 'Derby Crown Porcelain Company,' but in 1891 it acquired the prefix 'Royal' when a crown was added to its mark.

Throughout the period with which we are concerned the King Street factory produced a variety of dogs, sometimes in biscuit but usually glazed. Recorded examples of biscuit dogs include a pair of greyhounds (Colour Plate 2) and a recumbent spaniel (Colour Plate 125). Although some glazed dogs were decorated in enamel colours, most were left in the white, e.g. a standing pug (Colour Plate 27), a seated pug (Colour Plate 28), a group of three pugs (Colour Plate 29), a Pekingese (Colour Plate 226), a hound (Colour Plate 201), and a dachshund (Colour Plate 227). It has not been possible to determine with any precision the date of these white-glazed animals, but it can at least be safely stated that they were produced in the later part of the nineteenth century. Some have suggested a date of around 1890.

CHAMBERLAIN WORCESTER

The history of the Chamberlain Worcester factory has been exhaustively set out in Godden's *Chamberlain Worcester Porcelain* and the reader is referred to that work for a full exposition of the origin, development and eventual decline of this factory. However, it is enough for our purposes to state that Robert Chamberlain (1737–98), reputedly the first apprentice of the original 'Dr Wall' factory, rose to become head of the decorating department of that concern (then under the control of John and Joseph Flight); that in or about 1786, together with his son Humphrey, he left to establish his own decorating business, seemingly undertaking contract work for the Flights and embellishing porcelain from Thomas Turner of Caughley; that in June 1789, with the financial backing of Richard Nash and Thomas Turner, he opened a retail shop at 33 High Street, Worcester; and that from March 1791 or, at any rate, from the autumn of that year, he added to his decorating activities the actual manufacture of porcelain.

The business prospered from the beginning, and by the end of the eighteenth century the Chamberlain factory, now under the control of Humphrey Chamberlain, had attained a national, and possibly international, reputation. On 3 August 1807 the Royal Warrant as porcelain manufacturer to the Prince of Wales was granted (an honour publicised in some of the subsequent factory marks). On 25 May 1814 the Chamberlain firm was also appointed porcelain manufacturer to the Princess Charlotte of Wales, and it may be that by then it had surpassed the original Worcester factory, at that time trading as 'Flight, Barr and Barr'.

In June 1814 the Chamberlain concern opened its own London showrooms at 63 Piccadilly, and in July 1816 transferred from there to 155 New Bond Street. These addresses are sometimes incorporated into the factory's mark, thereby facilitating considerably the dating of specimens. In 1840 the Chamberlain concern merged with its chief rival at Worcester, still trading under the name of 'Flight, Barr and Barr'.

Joseph Flight had died in 1838 and thereafter his firm, under the exclusive control of Martin Barr and George Barr, declined, so that when the merger took place the Chamberlains were the senior partners. It was resolved 'that the manufactory shall be styled The Worcester Royal Pavilion Works but that the business shall be carried on under the Firm of Chamberlain and Co.'. From 1840 onwards the old mark 'Chamberlain' or 'Chamberlains', printed, painted or incised in script, was replaced by the words 'Chamberlain & Co.' similarly written. Incidentally, both the old and the new mark were, frequently, but not always, accompanied by the additional word 'Worcester', or very rarely 'Wor^{S}',[14] and sometimes by the address of Chamberlain's London Shop (taken over by the new amalgamated firm) until its sale in December 1845. Very rarely the address of Flight Barr and Barrs' showroom at 1 Coventry Street was added until its eventual disposal in December 1844. For the period from about 1847 to about 1852 the basic mark was changed again, this time to an impressed mark in the form of 'CHAMBERLAINS' in capital letters, sometimes with the word 'WORCESTER' similarly impressed.

Sadly the amalgamation was not a success. By 1852 all the original partners in the merger had died or retired, and the concern had come into the hands of a new partnership, Kerr & Binns. Under the new management the factory re-established its old standing, and in 1862 was formed into a company under the name 'Worcester Royal Porcelain Company', its subsequent products being known throughout the world as 'Royal Worcester'.

It is fortunate for the purposes of identification that many Chamberlain dogs were marked. Apart from the marks already referred to, reference should also be made to three rare marks (clearly applicable to a period before the merger). Two are in script: 'H Chamberlain and Sons Worcester', and 'Chamberlains Royal Porcelain Manufacturers'. The third rare mark, which appears under the base of a poodle illustrated by Godden,[15] is in the form of the elaborate printed Royal Arms mark together with the New Bond Street address.

The Chamberlain Worcester paste is somewhat grey in appearance, and is harsher than that of such factories as Rockingham, Derby and Minton.

Chamberlain animal dog bases assume various shapes. Sometimes they are rectangular, usually with rounded corners (e.g. Colour Plates 31, 32, 33 (top row) and 48), sometimes in the form of a cushion (e.g. Colour Plates 30b, 46 and 47) and sometimes stepped rectangular with canted corners (e.g. Colour Plates 202). They are generally recessed underneath. As for decoration, the bases were left in the white or given a dry-blue, green, or very rarely, a pink ground colour, and normally were edged with a gilt line. The dry-blue colour was apparently an expensive form of decoration. Godden points out in his *Chamberlain Worcester Porcelain* that where in the factory's priced listings the dry-blue colour appears, the factory price was greater than where this form of decoration was not used. The fact that the base was in a particular case left in the white did not preclude the animal itself being coloured.

An up-to-date list of the factory's dogs that have so far come to light is given below.

Description	Height	Length	Illustration
Recumbent greyhound	4in.		Figure 4
Pair of seated pugs on rectangular bases	2½/2⅝/2¾in.		Colour Plates 31, 32 and 33 (top)
Seated pug on a cushion base	2⅝in.		Colour Plate 30b
Standing poodle	1⅞in.	2in.	Colour Plate 50b
Seated poodle	2¾in.		Colour Plates 51 and 52

DESCRIPTION	HEIGHT	LENGTH	ILLUSTRATION
Poodle with rear upraised and basket in its mouth on a tasselled cushion		4in.	Colour Plate 46
As above, but with pricked ears		4in.	Colour Plate 47
As above, but with drooping ears, without basket, ridden by Cupid			
Poodle with rear upraised and basket in its mouth on a rectangular base with rounded corners		4in.	Colour Plate 48
Poodle with rear upraised and basket filled with fruit in its mouth		4in.	
Pointer	1¾in.	2in.	Colour Plate 189
Foxhound	2⅝in.		Colour Plate 202
Seated pug, left front paw upraised, recumbent puppy beside it, free-standing			

GRAINGER LEE & CO., WORCESTER

Just as Robert Chamberlain broke away from the old 'Dr Wall' factory and established a new concern, so similarly in 1801 Thomas Grainger, a painter at the Chamberlain works, and nephew of Humphrey Chamberlain, to whom he had been apprenticed, left his employers to found a new factory in St. Martin's Street, Worcester. However, at first he and his partner, an accomplished artist called Wood, did little more than decorate for re-sale porcelain purchased in the white. They traded as 'Grainger & Wood'. But in 1812 the factory was rebuilt and a new partnership was formed between Thomas Grainger and his brother-in-law, a certain Mr. Lee. The new concern traded as 'Grainger Lee & Co.'. It would seem that Lee retired in 1837, and that thereafter until his death in 1839 Thomas Grainger traded as 'Grainger & Co.'. On his demise he was succeeded by his son George Grainger, who added the initial 'G' to the trading name, making it 'G. Grainger & Co.'. The business lasted until 1889 when it was taken over by the Royal Worcester Company.

The factory's output was principally of useful ware, but it did manufacture some ornamental porcelain and, what is more germane to our subject, a certain number of small animals including dogs, identified by the impressed mark under the base 'GRAINGER LEE & CO., WORCESTER'[16] in capitals, or more rarely by the mark 'Grainger Lee & Co.' in red script, or, where the piece is unmarked, by the corresponding illustration in the factory pattern book. It would seem the factory ceased animal production after 1837. The commencement date is unknown, but as the factory was presumably in direct competition with Chamberlain, it probably began turning out dogs and other animals around 1820.

The paste of Grainger Lee animals is much whiter and less harsh than that of Chamberlain animals, and its glaze is much softer to the touch.

As can be seen from the illustrations, Grainger Lee bases vary in form. Most can be broadly described as being rectangular with rounded corners, but this is only a rough indication of the shape. Note the attractive rope feature shown in Colour Plate 221. The underside of the base is recessed and glazed. When the mark occurs – it appears under the base – it is often very faintly impressed and can, at a cursory glance, sometimes be missed. Grainger Lee dog models appear in biscuit (Colour Plate 53), in white and gilt (e.g. Colour Plate 3), and occasionally in enamel colours (e.g. Figure 25).

I have already referred in the previous chapter to the dogs which appear in the factory pattern book,[17] and where a porcelain model has been identified with a particular illustration, I have drawn attention to it. For convenience, the relevant models are set out in Part I of the list below. There are, however, in addition Grainger Lee dogs which do not appear in the pattern book. They are included in Part II, and, where they are here illustrated, an appropriate reference is made. The pattern book is dated October 1832, so that it is possible that the models not appearing there were produced after that date. On the other hand, of course, they could have been produced before October 1832, but for some reason simply omitted from the pattern book.

It is interesting to note that Henry and John Sandon in the course of their researches discovered a list of animals appearing (with prices) on an undated page of the factory's records, and these include the following dogs.[18]

PRICES OF ANIMALS NETT	GILT	COLOURED PROPER	PLAIN
Greyhound lying down	3/-	3/6	2/6
Indian hare dog	3/-	3/6	2/6
Spaniel standing	1/10	2/2	1/6
Tirrier [*sic*] lying	1/8	2/-	1/4
French poodle			1/4

Presumably those described as 'gilt' were white and gilt, those described as 'Coloured proper' were both gilded and decorated with enamel colours, and those described as 'plain' were simply glazed white. If this is right, there would seem to be no separate classification of biscuit examples. At Derby, and presumably other contemporary factories, biscuit items commanded a significantly higher price than decorated specimens.

The French poodle referred to above seems remarkably cheap if it is the version appearing either in the pattern book or in Colour Plate 53. Either poodle would seem to be about the same size as either of the greyhounds of Colour Plate 3.

Part I

DESCRIPTION	HEIGHT	LENGTH	ILLUSTRATION
Poodle on a tasselled cushion base supported on bun feet	3⅛in.		
Pair of recumbent greyhounds, one with head raised		4½in.	Colour Plates 3 and 8 (second row left)
Indian Hare dog standing (two sizes)		4¾/5⅛in.	Colour Plate 208 and Figure 24
Pointer trotting (in reverse to the setter illustrated in the pattern book)	2⅞in.	4¾in.	Colour Plate 190
Terrier sniffing a rat		5in.	Colour Plate 222

Part II

DESCRIPTION	HEIGHT	LENGTH	ILLUSTRATION
Poodle on a tasselled cushion base with a basket of flowers in its mouth		4in.	Colour Plate 53
Newfoundland standing	4¾in.	-	Figure 27
Indian hare dog lying recumbent with head raised		4⅝in.	Colour Plate 209 and Figure 25

DESCRIPTION	HEIGHT	LENGTH	ILLUSTRATION
Indian hare dog lying recumbent with head down (reverse of above)		4⅛in.	Figure 26
Terrier lying recumbent		3¼in.	Colour Plate 221
Great Dane lying recumbent		4¾in.	Figure 21

ROYAL WORCESTER

The Royal Worcester factory resumed the production of animal models, a speciality seemingly abandoned by the Chamberlain Worcester and Grainger Lee factories long before they became part of the new enterprise. Henry Sandon, a former curator of the Dyson Perrins Museum, has extracted[19] from the factory's records what purports to be the full range of its output, and this includes, for the period from 1862 to 1900, certain animal models, including dogs, although they represent only a small fraction of the totality of the models produced at Worcester. Some of these models were quite large, in fact on the Parian scale rather than the miniature scale of the small more collectable animals of the first half of the nineteenth century. Sometimes these animals were made in porcelain, sometimes in earthenware, The factory also turned out animals in Parian, sometimes glazed and tinted.

MINTON

In 1793 Thomas Minton (born 1765) founded the famous factory that today still bears his name, although it would appear from its records that he did not begin business until 1796. He had been apprenticed to Thomas Turner at the Caughley porcelain factory where he had learnt the art of engraving for the purposes of printing on ceramics. In 1796, together with William Pownall (a Liverpool merchant, who for a few years as a sleeping partner provided capital to extend the firm's operations) and Joseph Poulson (a practical potter, reputedly a former manager of the neighbouring Spode works), he began to manufacture blue printed pottery at Stoke. In about 1797 he added porcelain production. In November 1808 Joseph Poulson died and his expertise was made good by the employment of John Turner from the firm of John and William Turner of Lane End. Porcelain production continued until about 1816, when the factory reverted to pottery manufacture only. However, porcelain production was subsequently resumed. Although Jewitt writes of the recommencement date as being 1821,[20] Godden has shown by reference to the factory records that a more likely date was 1824. It has continued to the present day. There is no evidence to suggest that any porcelain animals were turned out in the first period of porcelain manufacture. They would all seem to be post-1830.

In 1817 Thomas Minton took into partnership his two sons, Thomas and Herbert, and traded under the name 'Thomas Minton & Sons'. However, after a while, Thomas, the elder brother, left to train for the church, becoming ordained in 1825, and on 1 January 1823 the 1817 partnership was dissolved. The new partners were Thomas and Herbert Minton, and on the former's death in 1836 Herbert became sole owner. Born on 3 February 1793 he had been in the ceramic trade since 1808, having been employed by his father, first as a traveller and salesman, and later in the factory itself.

By 1836 the business had grown to such an extent that Herbert felt obliged to take in a partner. His choice fell on John Boyle, an experienced and enthusiastic young man, and selected entries from the latter's diary give us a vivid insight into the events of the partnership. However, the relationship between Minton and Boyle degenerated, and in

1841 the partnership was dissolved. The business thereafter traded under the style of 'Herbert Minton & Co.'. In or before 1842 Michael Daintry Hollins became a partner – he had been employed in the business since at least December 1838 – receiving one-sixth of the profits, and in 1849 Colin Minton Campbell, Herbert Minton's nephew, was also taken in, receiving a third share of the profits. The latter two carried on the business after Herbert's death in 1858, although for some years previously he had retired from the day-to-day management of the firm.

Minton dogs appear in biscuit (e.g. Colour Plates 54 and 171) or glazed. In the latter case, they are either white and gilt (e.g. Colour Plates 34 and 210 and Figure 5), or enamelled and gilt (e.g. Colour Plates 4, 5, and 35). The paste can best be judged from biscuit specimens. It is very similar in colour and texture to that of the Rockingham and Derby factories, and, as in the case of these two concerns, the glaze is soft to the touch. The paste is quite unlike that produced by the Chamberlain Worcester company. After about 1847 Minton animals came to be made in Parian.

The structure of the underside of the base – flat and closed-in save for a small round hole occupying an approximately central position – is indistinguishable from that used to support Rockingham and Derby animals. Seemingly, this method of construction was introduced from Derby by Edward Keys who was also almost certainly responsible for modelling the early Minton animals. As is the case with Derby bases, but not Rockingham bases, there is never an incised number. Moreover, whilst a factory mark appears more often than not on Rockingham animals and sometimes, albeit rarely, on Derby animals, it never appears under the Minton counterparts.[21] In the case of later Minton animals (e.g. models 119 and 120) the underside of the base is hollow, similar to the products of the minor Staffordshire factories.

Fortunately, the factory's drawing book has survived, being now in the possession of the Minton Museum. With the aid of the illustrations which appear there, it has proved possible to identify the various animals, mainly dogs, that the factory turned out. Without these illustrations, the task would have been far from easy, because during the period when these animals were manufactured it was not the factory's practice to mark its products, seemingly in deference to the pressure imposed by the London and other retailers.

It is clear from the internal evidence of the drawing book that the dog models were made around late 1831 or 1832. Accordingly most examples will date from shortly afterwards, and few, if any, will have been produced after, say, 1840.

A list of Minton dogs, of which examples are recorded, is given below. Part I comprises those models appearing in the factory drawing book, Part II the models not shown in the drawing book.

Part I

No	Description	Height	Length	Illustration
18	Greyhound recumbent (i) on a tasselled cushion		4/4¼in.	Colour Plates 4 and 33 (second row right), Figure 5
	ii) on a rectangular base with rounded corners[22]		3⅝in.	Colour Plate 5
19	Poodle with a raised rear on a tasselled cushion, without a basket (reverse of No 33)		4in.	

No	Description	Height	Length	Illustration
20	Pug recumbent (i) on a tasselled cushion		4/4¼in.	Colour Plates 33 (second row left), and 34
	(ii) on a rectangular base with rounded corners[22]		3¾in.	Colour Plates 35 and 33 (third row)
21	Newfoundland standing	3⅝in.	5in.	Colour Plate 210
22	King Charles spaniel recumbent on a tasselled cushion		4in.	Colour Plate 128 and Figure 11
25	Newfoundland ridden by a boy representing 'war'		5in.[23]	
26	Newfoundland ridden by a girl representing 'peace'		5in.[23]	
31	Trotting pointer on mound base		3½in.	Colour Plate 191
33	Poodle with a raised rear on a tasselled cushion and with a basket in its mouth		4in.	Colour Plate 54
79	Dog with shepherd	7in.[23]		
87	Seated dog (possibly a pointer) and cat accompanying a seated man and woman as a group from Tom Jones		7½in.[23]	
112	Two dogs (one seemingly a setter, one a terrier) accompanying a kneeling gamekeeper		12½in.[23]	
119	Persian greyhound seated on a deep rocky base	7in.		Colour Plate 215
120	Greyhound seated on a deep rocky base	6½in.		Colour Plate 6
130	Large greyhound seated	13¾in.		

Part II

Description	Height	Length	Illustration
Setter recumbent			
(i) on a tasselled cushion		4½in.	Colour Plate 171
(ii) on a deep rectangular base		4⅛in.	Colour Plate 172
Pointer recumbent on a deep rectangular base		4¼in.	Colour Plate 192
Spill-holder with King Charles spaniel	5in.[24]		Colour Plate 129

Certain dogs appearing in the Drawing Book have not so far been recorded in porcelain, namely: King Charles spaniel begging (No 32), though it appears in the group of Colour Plate 129; the Russian dog on cushion (seemingly a borzoi, No 46); a boy playing with a dog (No 49); a wolf dog (seemingly 'the dog of Alcibiades', No 227); a group of two greyhounds on a rectangular base with canted corners (No 229).

COPELAND & GARRETT

On the death of Josiah Spode III in 1829, the famous factory, which had been founded by his grandfather in 1770, and carried on by his father (the latter had died only two years before Josiah III), was thereafter continued by his executors and one William Taylor Copeland, an Alderman of the City of London. As well as producing earthenware the factory turned out porcelain of a high order. On 1 March 1833 Copeland purchased the concern, and took into partnership Thomas Garrett, who had been Spode's principal traveller. The partnership lasted until the middle of 1847.

Copeland & Garrett, unlike the Spodes, introduced into their output small porcelain animals, including dogs. These are of fine quality, as would be expected of a factory that was one of the largest and most important in Staffordshire, having in 1840, according to John Ward, 800 employees and occupying an area of eight acres in the very centre of Stoke.[25] The factory usually marked its products, so that identification is easy. It was the practice of this factory, unlike that of the contemporary Derby and Minton factories, not to make the underside of the base of each animal flat, but instead to leave it recessed in a way similar to that normally adopted at the Chamberlain and Grainger Lee factories. The mark, when used on coloured figures, usually takes the form of the partnership name, Copeland & Garrett, printed in a circle within a circular wreath surmounted by a crown.

A list of Copeland & Garrett dog models so far recorded is set out below. It is interesting to note that, notwithstanding the popularity of the breed, no poodle is included.

	LENGTH	ILLUSTRATION
Large pair of greyhounds, each recumbent on a rectangular base with shaped corners	11in.	Figure 6
Pair of greyhounds, each recumbent on a shallow mound base	5in.	Colour Plate 7
Greyhound scratching, lying on a shaped rectangular base moulded with scrolls	5in.	Colour Plate 8 (first row)
Large recumbent King Charles spaniel on a rectangular base with rounded corners	8in.	
Large recumbent King Charles spaniel on a cushion base		
Large recumbent King Charles spaniel with three puppies on a cushion base		
Small King Charles spaniel recumbent on a shaped rectangular base moulded with scrolls	4½in.	Colour Plate 130
Large recumbent setter on a rectangular base	8in.	

COPELAND

On the retirement of Thomas Garrett in 1847 the partnership of Copeland & Garrett came to an end, and W.T. Copeland became sole proprietor. He thereafter traded as 'W.T. Copeland, late Spode', until 1867 when he took his four sons into partnership. The firm's name then became 'W.T. Copeland & Sons'.

Although Parian was in fact produced by the factory during the partnership of

Copeland & Garrett, it was not until after the death of Garrett that this body was used on a substantial scale. Parian was employed principally in the representation of statuary, but occasionally animals, including dogs, appear in this medium. They are, however, like the statuary, apt to be large and in consequence wholly different in spirit from the small, highly collectable animals of the first half of the nineteenth century. They are often impressed with the mark 'COPELAND'.

DAVENPORT

According to Alexander Brongniart, there was at the Davenport factory, which operated at Longport in Staffordshire from 1794 to 1887, a workforce in 1836 of some 1,400 persons with an annual output of £100,000 worth of pottery and porcelain.[26] The magnitude of such an output can be more readily comprehended if one bears in mind that in 1848 a dinner-set of light blue printed earthenware with gilt knobs and handles, for twenty-four persons, 220 pieces in all, was exported to India for a mere £16 less 10 per cent discount.[27] There can be little doubt that in 1836 the Davenport factory was the largest concern in Staffordshire. Its activities covered pottery, porcelain (both useful and ornamental), and glass. It exported its products to India, Rio de Janeiro, and throughout the world generally.

Now, in view of the range and magnitude of its activities, is it likely that it would have neglected figure production altogether? At least one marked figure has been discovered.[28] It consists of a boy in biscuit pushing a glazed wheelbarrow containing a glazed barrel. The barrel held ink, whilst next to it stood a receptacle for a quill. A particularly interesting feature was the rectangular base edged with a thick gilt line. However, no *marked animal*, and in particular no *marked dog*, has so far been discovered. But we know that from 1820 onwards, porcelain animals were being turned out in quantity in this country to meet a ready market. It is difficult to believe that the Davenport factory chose to ignore such a market. It may be that its output of porcelain animals was small, and that very few have survived. But it would be surprising if none had ever been made.

The admitted absence of a mark is not particularly startling. Much, if not most, of the Davenport output is unmarked. Moreover, some of the contemporary factories, such as Minton and Samuel Alcock, appear never to have marked their animals. Presumably the retail outlets preferred it this way.

If the Davenport factory did turn out small porcelain animals, we would expect to find them well modelled, heavy in weight, finely gilded and sometimes subject to crazing. These criteria are satisfied by the spaniel of Colour Plate 131 (note the gilt band around the base similar to that of the marked wheelbarrow figure), and the setter of Colour Plate 173. There are animals other than dogs which also have the above characteristics, but they lie outside the ambit of this book.

SAMUEL ALCOCK

Samuel Alcock began production of porcelain in about 1822 at Cobridge.[29] In 1834 he moved to the Hill Pottery at Burslem, and there developed one of the largest porcelain concerns of the early Victorian age.[30] His output was voluminous, but the quality, though often of a high order, was not generally comparable with that of the really great contemporary factories. However, the undertaking was throughout Alcock's life a great commercial success. His business philosophy was attacked in a letter in William Evans' penny weekly *The Potter's Examiner and Workman's Advocate*,[31] written by someone using the pseudonym 'Mentor'. The letter reveals that business was 'roaring' and that Alcock's products were inexpensive. Of them the writer says: '. . . cheap labour begets cheap goods; and he who can sell the cheapest will have the most orders. You have put this admirable practice into full operation, and have borne off the palm, for the present, for being the CHEAP SHOP of the Potteries. . .' Samuel Alcock was not alone in being attacked for paying low wages. *The Potter's Examiner* was concerned with establishing unions in the industry and with assisting the emigration of workers to America. It was pro-worker and anti-management.[32]

Samuel Alcock became a very prominent figure in local politics, but died in November 1848 at the early age of forty-nine. Thereafter the concern was carried on by his widow, Elizabeth, and her son Samuel, and Godden's researches have shown that in 1851, according to the Census, they employed a larger workforce than John Ridgway ('Potter to the Queen'). The comparative figures are as follows:

	Men	Women	Boys	Girls	Total
Alcock	249	187	135	116	687
Ridgway	230	162	154	74	620

However, in October 1859 the business became insolvent.

The range of Samuel Alcock's products was considerable including usefulware, fine quality biscuit busts and Parian statuary. However, the factory would never have been associated, in the mind of the present-day collector, with small animals including dogs, had it not been for the lucky chance that when, in April 1839, Samuel Alcock erected a new factory building, he arranged for a selection of the factory's products, including animals, to be placed under the foundation stone. Samuel Alcock animals are normally, though not invariably, impressed with an identifying numeral,[33] usually difficult to read and sometimes indecipherable. Some Samuel Alcock animals carry under the base a small asterisk, either impressed or printed in red. Other forms of marking are also sometimes found in the form of dots and other signs. The factory mark is often found on Parian groups containing an animal.

The standard of modelling varies considerably, perhaps not surprisingly, in view of the Mentor's reference to the factory as being the 'CHEAP SHOP of the Potteries'. Some Alcock dogs, however, whatever their technical shortcomings, are modelled with great vigour and are as charming as any dogs produced anywhere.

The colours applied to the bases of Samuel Alcock dogs are, where they are not simply left white, normally yellow or green, the latter colour being less frequent than the former. Although, for convenience, the description 'yellow' is used, in fact there are various gradations of colour covered by this term, ranging from deep cream to light and dark beige and then to progressively deeper shades of yellow. What were clearly intended as pairs are frequently found on 'yellow' bases of different tones. The factory also employed on some bases a dirty pink colour (fortunately this is seldom encountered), a cobalt blue and very rarely a pleasant light blue.

Samuel Alcock dog bases assume various shapes. Sometimes they are shallow (pad bases), sometimes they are deep (mound bases). These bases are normally moulded with intricate scrolling (e.g. Colour Plate 57), but are occasionally left plain without any scroll moulding whatsoever (e.g. Colour Plate 68). Often they are rocky in varying degrees (e.g. Colour Plates 193 and 198). Rarely the base is flat with shaped scrolled edges (No

13, Colour Plate 174).

A list of recorded Samuel Alcock dog models is given below. It must not be assumed that the vacant numbers are unidentified. In many cases they are impressed under animals other than dogs, under human figures (e.g. Dr. Syntax No 235), and sometimes under cottages or castles.

No	Description	Height	Length	Illustration
7	Pair of unclipped poodles with cropped ears standing on a rocky mound base	2¾in.		Colour Plate 61 and Figure 7
13	Recumbent setter on a scrolled base		5in.	Colour Plate 174
	Recumbent pointer on a scrolled base		5in.	
18 or 81[34]	Recumbent King Charles spaniel on a mound base with scrolled mouldings		3in.	Colour Plates 136 and 137
	Reverse model		3in.	
22	Poodle with basket in its mouth standing on a scrolled pad base	2¾in.		Colour Plate 62
25	Recumbent King Charles Spaniel on a mound base		2¼in.	Colour Plate 134a
36	Pair of poodles with upraised rears, lying on a scrolled mound base each with a bone in its mouth (sometimes without the bone)		3¼in.	Colour Plate 63
55	Group comprising a pair of chained greyhounds lying on a tasselled cushion		7¼in.	Colour Plate 12
93	Recumbent greyhound on mound base		4¼in.	Colour Plate 10
95	Pair of poodles, each recumbent with raised rear on a mound base, with meat or large bone in its mouth		4¾in.	Colour Plate 64
108	Pointer trotting beside a supporting tree on an oval rocky base		6¼in.	Colour Plate 193
121	Pair of King Charles spaniels, each seated on a mound base	4in.	5in.	Colour Plate 132
	Free-standing version of this model (i.e.without a base) unnumbered	4in.		Colour Plate 132
125[35]	King Charles Spaniels, seated	3in.		Colour Plate 133a
183[35]	Pair of King Charles Spaniels, each seated on an oval mound base		3/3⅛in.	Colour Plate 133b and Figure 13
192[36]	Wolf-dog standing on high rocky base	6in.		
201	Pair of greyhounds, each recumbent on a flat shaped rectangular mound base with scrolls		3½in.	Colour Plate 9
222	King Charles bitch seated, with two puppies standing on their hind legs playing	4¼in.		
231	Standing human figure with a standing Newfoundland dog	7½in.		

NO	DESCRIPTION	HEIGHT	LENGTH	ILLUSTRATION
239	Group comprising a cat playing with a seated poodle on a mound base	3½in.		Colour Plate 68
247	Unclipped poodle standing on mound base		3¼in.	Colour Plate 65
252	Recumbent poodle on a mound base		3½in.	Colour Plate 66
253[36]	Pair of wolf-dogs each seated on a high mound base	4in.		Colour Plate 224
266	Pug confronting on steps a cat with arched back. Also made in reverse	2¾in.		Colour Plates 37 and 38
305[37]	Pair of mastiffs, each lying recumbent on a rocky base		5½in.	Colour Plate 198
310	Pair of Dalmatians, each seated on a mound base	2¾in.		
311[38]	Saluki or Persian greyhound seated on a rocky mound base		3½in.	Colour Plate 214
311[38]	Begging poodle, wearing dunce's cap	4in.		Colour Plate 67
312	Pair of poodles, each seated upright on a scrolled mound base		3⅜in.	Colour Plates 57, 58 and 59a
323	Poodle clambering to eat out of a dish placed on a penholder		4in.	
329	Begging King Charles spaniel wearing a black hat on a mound base	4⅝in.		
342	Pug and King Charles spaniel seated on a scrolled mound base. Also made in reverse		3¼in.	Colour Plate 36

UNNUMBERED

DESCRIPTION	HEIGHT	LENGTH	ILLUSTRATION
Pair of poodles seated upright on scrolled mound bases in a slightly different pose to that of the dogs numbered 312	3⅝in. -		Colour Plates 59b and 60
What appears to be a setter sitting upright on a base similar to, but less sharply moulded than that supporting the Saluki numbered 311	3⅜in.		Colour Plate 175
Toy spaniel seated upright on an octagonal base moulded with leaves	1¾in.		Colour Plate 135
Large greyhound in biscuit recumbent on a glazed and enamelled base with the name Echo' along the front	8¼in.		Colour Plate 11
Parian group comprising a hound feeding or drinking from a dish held by a girl	7½in.		
Parian boy about to mount a Newfoundland	6in.		Colour Plate 213

INCORRECTLY NUMBERED

NO	DESCRIPTION	HEIGHT	LENGTH	ILLUSTRATION
2[39]	King Charles spaniel seated upright on a heavily scrolled mound base	2¼in.		Colour Plate 134b

In addition, the following models which are described in the relevant sale catalogues as Rockingham, but are nothing of the sort, may be from the Samuel Alcock factory:

'A Rockingham Figure of a Dalmatian, sleepily emerging from his kennel, surrounded by a border of green moss, gilt line-edged base, 2¼in. *impressed number 142*';[40] 'A Rockingham group of a Poodle and its Puppy, lying on a green and cream coloured cushion with tassels at the corner, 4¼in., *impressed numeral 330*.[41] Probably Alcock is 'A pair of Staffordshire figures of seated hounds, on yellow mound bases, their white bodies with grey markings, and with pointed noses, gilt edged rims, 3½in. *impressed numerals* 118 and 252'.[42]

'Hounds' would seem to be used as a generic term equal to 'dogs' and not a specific breed, for 252 appears in the Alcock list as a poodle. What breed 118 is, it is impossible to say.

CHARLES BOURNE

The Charles Bourne factory, which flourished at Foley in Staffordshire from about 1817 to 1830, was very much a minor concern in relation to the factories already mentioned. It is distinguishable from the general run of minor Staffordshire producers of good quality porcelain by the practice (not normally adopted elsewhere in Staffordshire) of sometimes marking its output. Its products are on occasion painted under the base with the letters 'C B', the initials of its proprietor Charles Bourne, and this has enabled us to identify a few animals as belonging to the factory, including a pug (Colour Plate 30a), a poodle and a pair of greyhounds (Colour Plate 15). The colour of the bases was normally white, green or blue.

It is interesting to note that the Charles Bourne factory was offered for sale or letting in November 1830 in the *Staffordshire Sentinel*:

> CHINA AND EARTHENWARE/MANUFACTORY/AT THE FOLEY, NEAR LANE END. To be Let or Sold by Private Contract, all these extensive and convenient premises consisting of three biscuit and three glost ovens with hardening and enamelling kiln and kiln room to make thereby thirty tons of clay a week'.
>
> Also the very substantial dwelling house, coach-house, stables and barn, with five acres of land, adjoining the canal company's railways with gardens, pleasure grounds, etc., complete now in possession of Mr. Charles Bourne, the proprietor, who is declining business on account of ill-health.

The fact that manufacture closed down by 1830 enables us to give a terminal date to the factory's production. Interestingly, it ceased operations at the same time as the Rockingham factory discontinued figure production. Broadly speaking, Charles Bourne and Rockingham dogs can be regarded as contemporaneous.

LLOYD SHELTON

John Lloyd, who was born around 1803, ran, with his wife Rebecca, some two years his senior, a small pottery and porcelain factory at Marsh Street, Shelton. The factory operated from about 1834 to 1852. On John's death, the business was carried on by his widow alone. They produced figures and toys generally, including animals, and more specifically dogs.

It is doubtful whether the work of John and Rebecca Lloyd would ever have been identified or, for that matter, their very existence been anything to us other than a mere name, had it not been for the very unusual fact that, contrary to the general practice of Staffordshire manufacturers, they did occasionally impress the bases of their figures with the name-make 'LLOYD/SHELTON'.

Various human figures with this mark have come to light, and their characteristics have to a limited extent enabled us to identify certain animal models including dogs.[43] The quality of the dogs so far identified with the Lloyd Shelton factory has been high. Examples are illustrated in Colour Plates 69–72.

MADELEY

Our knowledge of the porcelain produced at the Madeley factory in Shropshire between about 1828 and 1840 stems almost entirely from an article appearing in two parts in *The Connoisseur* of 1908 as amplified by Roger S. Edmunson in his article 'China Painter to the Local Worthy'.[44] The writer in *The Connoisseur* was W. Turner and he seems to have obtained his information from John Randall, the nephew of the proprietor, Thomas Martin Randall (1786–1859) John Randall was ninety-eight years of age at the time – he lived a further two years dying in 1910 – and was still in possession of his mental faculties. He had worked at the factory and was able to describe its activities and identify certain of its products which are illustrated in *The Connoisseur* article.

Apart from the considerable quantities of Sèvres porcelain which the factory imported, either in the white or slightly decorated – it could remove any existing decoration 'by the application of hydrofluoric acid' – and which it decorated in the Sèvres style,[45] it also produced its own porcelain. This was of two kinds: 'The one was soft paste very similar to "Nantgarw", "Old Swansea", and "Old Sèvres"; the other was a comparatively hard body. In its soft paste [the Madeley factory] strove to rival the French and meet the taste of the wealthy connoisseur; in the hard body, the wants of the general public were studied'.

Figures including animals, and in particular dogs, were manufactured at Madeley, but apparently 'not to any extent'. However, some were produced and from the harder body 'in which [Thomas Randall] would put a large proportion of Cornish china clay and stone'. Thomas Randall used 'Cornish clay (Kaolin), Cornish stone (petuntse), flint and potash', but no calcined bones. Nevertheless, it would seem that the paste was 'not the real true hard paste'. This is apparent from the way in which the colour decoration adhered to the glaze, not so closely as in the case of soft porcelain, but more so than in the case of true hard porcelain.

An illustration of one of the factory's dogs in *The Connoisseur* article is of a King Charles spaniel lying on a cushion. Seemingly, it belonged to John Randall himself, who guaranteed its authenticity. It is described as follows:

> Figure subject. Dog (modelled by Philip Ballard); on cushion as base; hard porcelain; white colour relieved with brown tints upon head, ears and tail. Base 3½in. long by 2½in. broad; dog 2in. long by 1½in. heigh. Unmarked.

Another example of this model, which has a bright-blue base, is shown in Figure 14.[46]

A pivotal piece for identifying Madeley animals – the factory, with only one recorded exception, appears never to have marked its products – is a billy goat 3⅝in. long (Colour Plate 216). It is made of an essentially hard body, and lies recumbent on a deep rocky base decorated with a distinctive turquoise-blue ground colour, closed-in underneath Of the turquoise-blue, W. Turner wrote in his *Connoisseur* article:

> A thin, hard glaze would not hold a thick mass of colour and hence the hard paste at Madeley never had the deep rich colour of the soft paste. The turquoise upon it (the hard paste) was thin and 'husky' looking – more like what at Coalport they called the 'bleu-celeste'.

And he went on to say:

> The ground colours were not so bright and delicate upon the hard paste because the glaze was also hard and would not amalgamate with the colour in the process of firing, especially the turquoise and green; but maroon, pink and Rose du Barry succeeded upon it.

The Persian greyhound or saluki illustrated in Colour Plate 216 would also appear to come from the Madeley factory. The porcelain of the animal corresponds exactly with that of the goat, as does the grey decoration. The base is embellished with splashes of turquoise and is edged with a continuous apple-green line. The turquoise ranges in intensity from pure turquoise to the 'blue-celeste' version on the base of the goat. As explained in *The Connoisseur* article, owing to the hardness of the glaze the enamels do not completely sink in. The dog illustrated in Colour Plate 216 measures 5in. long by 2¾in. wide. Another example of this model but somewhat larger, measuring 6in. long by 3¼in. wide, is shown in Colour Plate 217. The dog is decorated in a heavy brown, which does not fully sink into the glaze. Each dog has a base whose underside is, in the manner of Rockingham, Derby and early Minton, closed-in except for a centrally located hole.

It is interesting to note that a Persian greyhound was included among the animals kept at the Regent's Park Zoological Gardens, being exhibited there for the first time in 1831.

That Philip Ballard was responsible for modelling the dog of Figure 14 is established by the evidence of John Randall. But any doubt there might be is dispelled by the discovery on the part of Roger S. Edmunson, who had the good fortune of talking to two great nephews of Philip Ballard, of an old label under the dog he illustrates in his article, inscribed in two hands 'Uncle Philip's dog – modelled by Uncle Philip'. Conceivably, Philip Ballard modelled all the factory's animals, but it must be borne in mind that, according to Turner's *Connoisseur* articles there was another modeller working permanently at the factory – F. Brewer.

Thomas Martin Randall left Madeley to continue his business in Shelton, where he was approached by Herbert Minton, who admired his porcelain, with an invitation to work for him, but he declined.[47] It is interesting to note that Thomas Martin Randall appears as trading in Shelton in Kelly's *Post Office Directory* for 1850. Philip Ballard left Madeley in 1833. For his subsequent career see 'China Painter to Local Worthy'.[44]

DUDSON

James Dudson was born around 1813 in Shelton. Jewitt, after remarking that the business had been established in 1800, says as follows:

> In 1835 Mr. James Dudson entered upon the works, and they are still carried on by him. [He in fact died in 1882, but the concern exists today, trading as Dudson Bros. at the original address, Hope Street, Hanley.] At one time he manufactured ornamental china figures, vases and services . . . Mr. Dudson, who received 'honourable mention' in the Exhibitions of 1851 and 1862, supplies both home and foreign markets.[48]

The items entered in the 1851 Exhibition by James Dudson were 'ornamental china figures'.

Audrey Dudson, in her informative book *Dudson: A family of potters since 1800*, has pointed out that although the factory was predominantly a producer of earthenware –

both a very white firing earthenware and also the common earthenware – some of its output was also manufactured in porcelain. Indeed, the same figure model may be found in all three bodies. Moreover it is thought that the later models were also made in Parian. From the factory records Mrs. Dudson has listed the various animal models emanating from the factory,[49] but has been unable to say positively that any particular model was, for certain, produced in porcelain. All figure production declined after about 1850 and ceased altogether around 1865. Since Mrs. Dudson wrote her book (1985), excavations have taken place on site, and a group of three red spaniels seated on a blue quill-holder base has come to light (Figure 15). This particular item is in earthenware, but Mrs. Dudson believes that the model could just as well have appeared in porcelain.

Certain shards excavated from the site have been found by Mrs. Dudson and Mrs. Delia Napier to correspond with the bases of the pair of poodles (each with a large impressed asterisk) illustrated in Colour Plate 73. It is interesting to note that the animals were not always so positioned that the front was in line with the side of the base with the more elaborate scrolling. Those animals with this type of base can be confidently ascribed to the Dudson factory. So too can the poodle groups of Colour Plate 74. For once again these have been identified with wasters from the factory site. It may also be the case that the group of animals referred to below on this page are also attributable to the Dudson factory.

It is to be hoped that in the course of time, with the help of excavations carried out on the site, it will be possible to attribute other models to the Dudson factory.

UNIDENTIFIED STAFFORDSHIRE FACTORIES

Although it is impossible, on the present state of our knowledge, to identify those dogs styled here 'Staffordshire' with any particular factory or factories, certain models clearly have the same factory of origin, whatever factory that may be. Thus the straight-backed poodle of Colour Plate 89 which is sometimes accompanied by three puppies (Colour Plate 88), and which normally has an arch-backed poodle as a companion,[50] corresponds to the straight-backed hound of Colour Plate 203.[51] (The differences in the dog modelling, e.g. the absence of wool on the hound, are only such as serve to distinguish the breeds.) And the hound with an arch-back (Colour Plate 203) corresponds to the poodle with an arch-back. The poodle with three puppies corresponds to the pointer and three puppies of Colour Plate 195. Moreover, the basket-weave base of the latter ties in with the basket- weave base of the King Charles spaniel and puppies of Colour Plate 155. Manifestly, all these models[52] come from the same factory.

The straight-backed hound of Colour Plate 204, corresponding to the straight-backed hound of Colour Plate 203, has a base decorated with a distinctive combination of colours. The palette consists of brown, yellow/cream and green, brown predominating. The same palette has been identified by Mrs. Dudson, with further researches by Mrs. Napier, on the bases of a set of four seasons made by the Dudson factory in the 1840s and given to a member of the Dudson family. This set of seasons has recently returned to this country, and as a result the identification has been made possible.[53] If this identification is correct, then all the animals described above as being linked to one another will also be from the Dudson factory.

Another group of dogs with a common factory of origin have as their distinctive feature a shaped scroll base. Examples on bases 3½/3⅝in. long are a greyhound on a green base (Colour Plate 18), a parti-coloured poodle on a dark orange base (Colour Plate 96), and a King Charles spaniel on a turquoise base (Colour Plate 147). The more attractive side of the base is not always at the front.

A similar but more elaborate base is sometimes found where the dog, likewise recumbent, is invariably larger. The following examples are recorded: a setter (Colour Plates 176 and 177),[54] a companion pointer in reverse (Colour Plate 194), and a poodle (Colour Plates 94 and 95). Whether the factory responsible for the smaller dogs of Colour Plates 18, 96 and 147 also produced the larger animals is unknown.

The larger and more elaborate scrolled base referred to above would appear to have been derived from Derby models (Colour Plates 169, 170 and 188).[55] This style of base would seem to have been short-lived, a subject of fashion, and was probably in vogue from around 1837 to 1840.

Other dog models having no obvious connection with each other can, nevertheless, be linked to one another by reason of features shared with other animals (not necessarily dogs) having a common factory of origin.

It is possible by discovering a connection between various groups of dogs to assign them to factory A, B, C, D, etc., as appropriate, but as we do not know the identity of such factories, the exercise does not really lead us very far.

References

Introduction

1. Porcelain animals disappear from the scene, and the factories responsible for their production seem thereafter to have confined themselves to *pottery* figures only, and even these appear to tail away after about 1870, by which time the competitive effect of 'fairings' imported from Germany was being felt.
2. Youatt, p.98.

Dog Models and their Factories of Origin

1. Wynkyn de Worde, *The Treatise perteyning to Hawkynge, &c, emprynted at Westmestre*, 1496.
2. Youatt, p.36. There were by the middle of the nineteenth century 350 coursing clubs.
3. Bewick, p.296.
4. Taplin wrote, about the beginning of the nineteenth century, extensively and in depth on the characteristics of the dog.
5. Taplin's *The Sportsman's Cabinet*, 1803, includes twenty-four fine copperplate engravings by John Scott after the animal artist Philip Reinagle, R.A., in addition to numerous vignettes by Thomas Bewick.
6. Darton, p.166.
7. See the engraving of 1835 reproduced in Hutchinson, p.1003.
8. National Gallery, London.
9. Ashmolean Museum, Oxford.
10. National Gallery of Canada, Ottawa.
11. Louvre, Paris
12. Metropolitan Museum of Art, New York.
13. Sotheby's sale catalogue, 12 November 1968, Lot 96.
14. Haslem, p.179.
15. Reproduced in *The Connoisseur*, Vol. 45, 1916, p.197.
16. Christie's sale catalogue, 15 June 1970, Lot 173.
17. Nos. 65 and 120 in Haslem's numbered list, pp.172, 173.
18. Sotheby's sale catalogue, 20 December 1977, Lot 175. Presumably the base was the same as that of the hound of Colour Plate 202.
19. Godden, 1982, pp.213, 214; December 1813 and July 1824 respectively.
20. See Sandon, 1978, Appendix 1.
21. *Art Union*, December 1846.
22. ibid, May 1847.
23. And also on a long narrow flower-encrusted base to form a paperweight, as was also the case with the factory's pug, poodle and King Charles Spaniel (cf. Figure 12, p.85.).
24. Battie, p.56.
25. Unless the group in the Exhibition was a later version of the same subject.
26. They are also found in porcelain.
27. They were modelled at the Royal Worcester factory in 1862, 1872, 1873 and 1875.
28. A pug dog features in Jane Austin's *Mansfield Park* as the inseparable companion of Lady Bartram.
29. However, Hogarth illustrates a black pug in his 'The House of Cards'. Another appears in Nicholas de Largillière's 'Louis XIV and His Heirs'.
30. The suggestion has been made that this dog is not a pug, but some form of mastiff. The Chelsea animal is modelled after a terracotta by Roubiliac of Hogarth's dog Trump, lying in a recumbent position. The terracotta was sold after the death of the painter's widow in 1789 and was illustrated in an engraving in Samuel Ireland's *Graphic Illustrations of Hogarth*, published in 1799. It has since vanished. That Trump was a pug is manifest from his portrait alongside his master in Hogarth's painting of 1745, now in Tate Britain, although in fairness it may be that the animal was not pure bred but contained an element of mastiff. Hogarth had three pug dogs in succession, one of which actually answered to the name of 'Pugg' – see the advertisement inserted by Hogarth on 5 December 1730 in *The Craftsman* seeking the dog's return and offering a half guinea reward.
31. Youatt, p.166.
32. It is interesting to speculate who might have supplied the copy moulds to the Rockingham factory. It could not have been Coffee himself, as by the time the Rockingham factory began manufacture in 1826, Coffee had left this country and settled in America. Perhaps George Cocker supplied them.
33. An example of the largest size (a bitch) was exhibited at the Antique Porcelain and Pottery and Glass Fair, Cumberland Hotel, London, 24–26 February 1984.
34. Assuming that they did not turn out both versions concurrently. To complicate matters, a further Rockingham pug has come to light which, although essentially identical in shape and size with the later pug, has, instead of the collar with bells, a plainer version with an ordinary buckle fastening. The sole example known is white-glazed and 2⅝in. high. Although it is unmarked and unnumbered, its Rockingham provenance is established by its paste and glaze.
35. Haslem, p.178.
36. Illustrated Sotheby's sale catalogue, 25 March 1974, Lot 169.
37. The same numbering system was used in connection with Derby squirrels, foxes, deer, swans

and recumbent cats without bases, the last mentioned being only in two sizes, '1' and '2'.
38. Sotheby's sale 'British and Irish Ceramics', 22 May 1984, Lot 584.
39. Christie's sale, 15 October 1973, Lot 147.
40. Examples can be seen in Rice 1989, Figure 151.
41. A pair is illustrated in Rice 1983, Plate 77.
42. Interestingly, what appears to be the same model is also recorded on an oval base, Sotheby's sale, 25 March 1974, Lot 158.
43. Godden, 1982, p.213.
44. *The Connoisseur*, August 1918, Vol. 51, p.XXIX.
45. Godden, 1982, p.214.
46. This was produced in earthenware.
47. Illustrated Christie's South Kensington catalogue, 'English and Continental Ceramics', 23 January 1907, Lot 48.
48. Mary Browne (1807–33), *The Diary of a Girl in France in 1821*, 1905, entry for 7 May.
49. In the Wallace Collection.
50. Woburn Abbey. Attributed to the School of Gheeraerts.
51. In the Wallace Collection.
52. Secord, Plate 177.
53. ibid., Colour Plate 100.
54. Originally I thought it read 'No 82' and so stated in Rice 1989, Figure 37.
55. The base is in the same form as that of the factory's sheep model No 98, the model which, in the figure series, immediately follows the poodle.
56. Illustrated in *The Connoisseur*, 1915, Vol. 42, p.218, Plate IX, although it was not there given a Rockingham attribution.
57. Haslem, pp.179, 181.
58. Cf. the Samuel Alcock poodles of Colour Plate 61 and Figure 7.
59. Illustrated in Godden 1982, Colour Plate XIII.
60. Another example, on a green base with a tooled gilt border, appeared in the Phillips' sale of 15 December 1999, Lot 150. It was incised 'Chamberlains Royal Porcelain Worcester'.
61. An example on a pink base was sold by Phillips on 6 June 1996, Lot 792. What seems to be the same model but on an *oval* base appeared at Christie's South Kensington sale, The Boothman Smallwood Collection, 26/27 April 1989, Lot 964.
62. 'Toy' is used throughout this book as a description of the size of the porcelain dog, not as a reference to a technical sub-division of a particular breed.
63. Note that the base, which is completely closed in underneath is essentially the same as that of the dog of Colour Plate 189.
64. Godden, 1982, p.214.
65. Sandon, 1989, Plate 157.
66. A fine Chamberlain poodle illustrated in Godden, 1982, Colour Plate XIII, holds in its mouth a basket filled with fruits.
67. An example of model No 19 (said to be after a Vincennes model) appeared at the Exhibition of Staffordshire Porcelain 1740–1851 organised by the Northern Ceramics Society in 1979, and is illustrated in Plate 119 of the catalogue. The base was purple and yellow. Another example is shown in Jones. It lies on a tasselled cushion base decorated in crimson/purple and yellow).
68. A pair of poodles of this same model, but this time standing on a different style of base (hitherto unrecorded) from that of Colour Plate 65, was exhibited at the Olympia Antiques Fair of 1996. The mound bases were essentially rectangular with slightly concave sides and with some sparse scrolling by way of decoration.
69. 'Collecting Antique China and Pottery Dogs', *The Connoisseur*, 1915, Vol. 42, p.217, Plate No VII.
70. Illustrated in Oliver, 1971, Colour Plate 3.
71. An example is illustrated in Oliver, 1981, Plate 157.
72. The same model in reverse, but with more elaborate gilding on the base appears in Oliver, 1981, Plate 155.
73. An exception is the pair of Colour Plate 106 where the poodles hold game in their mouths.
74. Christie's South Kensington sale, 3 April 1997, Lot 198.
75. Battie, p.77.
76. The group shown in Hughes, p.185, has the bitch in its clipped version. Compare also Colour Plate 89.
77. They may possibly be Dudson products, see p.174.
78. See the example illustrated in Barrett and Thorpe, Plate 127.
79. Vivian, Figure 155.
80. However, the straight-backed poodle was sometimes simply reversed to make a pair.
81. An example of this same basic group is recorded where a dog of another breed replaces the poodle. In a further example the poodle is transposed, appearing in diminutive size on a raised platform to the boy's left.
82. See reference 62 above.
83. The spaniel appearing in the plaque would appear to be after an illustration in Taplin.
84. See Bradley, plate 42.
85. But see the pair of biscuit greyhounds illustrated in Colour Plate 2.
86. Godden, 1982, p.214.
87. Uffizi, Florence.
88. Woburn Abbey.
89. Yale Center for British Art, New Haven, Connecticut; and reproduced in *Apollo*, November 1987, p.328, plate 10.
90. Sold Sotheby's, 24 February 1987, Lot 250.
91. Another example is illustrated in an article by Roger E. Edmunson 'China Painter to Local Worthy', *Antique Dealer and Collectors' Guide*, March 1999, p.33. The same model – the modeller

was Philip Ballard – appears in *The Connoisseur*, 1908. See p.172.
92. See p.173–174.
93. Wood, p.290.
94. Youatt, p.91.
95. Bewick, p.313.
96. It is very like the Derby setter of Figure 17 (p.105). Was it based on it?
97. An example is recorded with the Bloor mark. It is interesting to note that this model, together with the companion pointer, was also produced in pottery in Staffordshire; see the illustration in Sotheby's sale catalogue, 25 March 1974, Lots 38, 39.
98. Cf. Godden, 1968, Plates 128, 129, 140, 142, 145 and 146.
99. See, for example, the illustration in Sotheby's sale catalogue, 6 December 1977, Lot 214.
100. Looking in the same direction as the greyhound bitch of Figure 6 (p.16).
101. It is assumed that the numbers, broadly at least, indicate the chronological order in which they were first produced.
102. National Gallery, London.
103. Haslem, p.179.
104. See for example Sotheby's sale, 'English Pottery and Porcelain', 18 May 1982, Lot 177.
105. See pp.105, 106.
106. Another example from the same factory was sold at Phillips, 15 December 1999, Lot 154.
107. Although such an achievement is far from unique; see, for example, the Rockingham setter of Colour Plate 167.
108. Query whether such pointer and setter were also made to lie on the rectangular base with rounded corners shown in Colour Plates 5, 33 (third row) and 35?
109. An illustration of such a pointer, 5in. long, can be seen in Godden, 1983, Plate 47.
110. This model may in fact be from the Dudson factory, see p.174.
111. Sotheby's sale catalogue, 3 October 1972, Lot 35.
112. Interestingly, a mastiff was at one time exhibited at the Regent's Park Zoo, London, first appearing in 1828.
113. In the Royal Collection.
114. Illustrated in Ritchie.
115. Battie, p.41
116. Vivian, Plate 155, p.187.
117. See pp.174.
118. Wood, pp. 295, 297.
119. See, for example, Rice 1983, Plate J.
120. Youatt, p.61.
121. Erroneously described in Rice 1989 as a Shepherds' Dog. It is in fact an Indian Hare Dog.
122. See p.163.
123. Ash, pp.17–19.
124. Grant, p.14.
125. Letter dated 3 December 1826.
126. See *The Connoisseur*, September 1922, p.34, illustration 11.
127. An example in biscuit can be seen in Godden 1968, plate 137. The base is oval with some raised mouldings around the edges, features which occur on the rectangular base of the setter of Colour Plate 172.
128. Whether the Minton factory also produced a companion in reverse is not known.
129. See Rice 1989, Figure 115.
130. The painting was reproduced in *The New Sporting Magazine* in 1837; see also Secord Colour Plate 132.
131. Letter dated 16 December 1827.
132. Frith, p.322.
133. In the same way that the factory sometimes omitted the saucer from the Rockingham cat and three kittens group (No 107).
134. See Sandon, 1989, p.158.
135. Published 1831, Vol.1, pp.258, 259.
136. Somewhat surprisingly the London Zoo formerly had on show a variety of English domestic dogs. These appear in Flower, Vol. I *Mammals*, with the date against each breed from which they were first exhibited. They include Alpine Mastiff 1835 or 1836, Bloodhound 1828, Mount St. Bernard 1839, Newfoundland 1840, Persian Greyhound 1831, Terrier 1828, Thibet [*sic*] Mastiff or Watch Dog 1828.
137. Mary Boyle, *Her Book*, London, 1901, pp.56, 57. It is clear from the context of the event described that Mary Boyle (1810–90) was still a child. She had three brothers born respectively in 1800, 1806 and 1814. Seemingly the event occurred in the early 1820s.
138. A gigantic Irish wolfhound is painted by Van Dyck beside Thomas Wentworth, later Earl of Strafford.
139. For a full account of the 'Dog of Alcibiades', see the exhibition catalogue, *The Treasure Houses of Britain*, National Gallery of Art, Washington, 1985, pp.318–319. The statue was acquired by the British Museum, London, in 2001.
140. National Gallery, London.
141. National Gallery, London.

The History and Output of the Factories

1. The griffin was the heraldic emblem of Earl Fitzwilliam, which the latter allowed the factory to use as part of its mark.
2. They almost certainly stand for 'class', see Cox, p.61.
3. However, the setter shown in Colour Plate 165, though gilt *and* enamelled, has the 'Cl 1' mark.
4. To complicate matters, very occasionally the factory made a mistake and incised the wrong number. Thus, the setter of Colour Plate 165 is incised 'No 90' instead of 'No 94'.

5. Where seemingly only '1' and '2' were used. Interestingly, in the case of cat models the explanatory word 'size' or 'siz' is occasionally found incised against the relevant number.
6. A contrary view has been expressed by Dr. Alwyn and Mrs. Angela Cox but, in my judgement this interpretation simply cannot stand in the face of the evidence as a whole. For a discussion of this issue see Appendix A of Rice 1989.
7. But see p.26.
8. See Rice, 1983, pp.9–22.
9. For his subsequent career see the article by Robin and Ross Barkla, *Derby Porcelain International Society Journal* 3, pp.26 *et seq.*
10. For a more detailed history of the factory's later period see Haslem, pp.15–31.
11. Those of the second half are dealt with under the King Street factory.
12. Haslem, p.217.
13. ibid., p.219.
14. Usually written in script underneath.
15. Godden 1983, Colour Plate XIII.
16. The word 'WORCESTER' is generally impressed underneath the trade name.
17. Dogs and other animals illustrated in the pattern book are reproduced in Rice 1989, pp.233–237.
18. See Sandon, 1989, p.158.
19. Sandon, 1978, Appendix I.
20. Jewitt, Vol. II, p.192.
21. The Minton mark is, however, often impressed on the base of later Parian animals.
22. Although the animal appears in the drawing book, this particular base does not.
23. Height of the group, not the animal.
24. Height of the group, not the spaniel. The spaniel is the dog No 32.
25. According to the *Report on the Employment of Children in Factories* of Samuel Scriven of 1843, appointed by the Government to inquire into the state of children employed in the pottery industry, the Copeland & Garrett factory employed 454 men, 249 women and 77 children, see Dudson 1999.
26. Alexander Brongniart, *Traité des Arts Ceramiques*, Vol II, 1836, p.453, quoted in Wedgwood.
27. Lockett, p.21.
28. 'Staffordshire Porcelain 1740–1851', exhibition catalogue, 1979, Plate 119.
29. An interesting reference to Samuel Alcock can be found in Cooper, p.200.
30. According to Chaffer, *Pottery and Porcelain*, 4th ed., 1968, p.668, the factory's modeller was M. Protat.
31. Saturday, 11 May 1844.
32. Godden, 1983, p.308.
33. Unfortunately, as in the case of the Rockingham factory, the wrong number was sometimes used.
34. Unfortunately, the reading of the number depends on which way up the dog is held. The problem does not arise in the case of Rockingham dogs, because there the number is prefixed by the letters 'No' and accordingly, it is obvious how the numeral should be viewed.

As presumably the whole object of numbering was to enable the factory to recognise the particular model corresponding to the number, the exercise would seem to have been thwarted by ambiguity
35. 125 may be mistake for 183, see pp.89, 90.
36. Model 192 was a larger version of model 253.
37. These are found in biscuit as well as in enamel colours.
38. Unfortunately, the factory made a mistake. The two models cannot both be 311, but in the absence of further specimens it is impossible to say which is right.
39. Presumably the number was incomplete.
40. Sotheby's sale catalogue, 3 October.1972, Lot 35.
41, Sotheby's sale catalogue, 3 October 1972, Lot 28.
42. Sotheby's sale catalogue, 3 February 1970, Lot 40.
43. See pp.55.
44. Roger S. Edmunson, 'China Painter to the Local Worthy', *The Antique Dealer and Collectors' Guide*, March 1999, pp.32–35. The first part of W. Turner's article in *The Connoisseur* was published in September 1908, p.153 *et seq.*, the second the following December, p.248 *et seq.* Subsequent quotes in the Madeley section are from *The Connoisseur* article.
45. This was the source of the greater part of the factory's earnings.
46. A further one appears in Roger S. Edmundson's article, p.33, see 44 above. The colour illustration also indicates a bright blue base but the author of the article refers to the dog so illustrated as lying on a turquoise base.
47. Jewitt, Vol. I, p.303.
48. Jewitt, Vol. II, p.336.
49. Dudson, 1985, Appendices D and E.
50. However, sometimes it has simply a reverse model.
51. The similarity relates, of course, to the dog, not the bases.
52. And others which are not dogs and therefore outside the scope of this book
53. The set descended to a grand-daughter, living in Australia, of the original donee, who has generously given them to the Dudson Museum.
54. Compare the similar base employed by Samuel Alcock (Colour Plate 174).
55. The underside of the base of the Derby model, however, is not left open but is closed-in save for a centrally located hole (Colour Plate 170b).

Selected Bibliography

(Published in London unless otherwise indicated)

Ash, Edward C.
The New Book of the Dog, 1938

Bambery, Anneke, and Blackwood, Robin
Derby Porcelain: The Factory at King Street (1849–1935).
Barrett, F.A., and Thorpe, A.L.
Derby Porcelain, 1971
Battie, David
Guide to Understanding 19th and 20th Century British Porcelain, 1994
Bemrose, William
Bow, Chelsea and Derby Porcelain, 1898
Bewick, Thomas
A General History of Quadrupeds, Newcastle-upon-Tyne, 1790
Bradley, H.G. (ed.)
Ceramics of Derbyshire 1750–1975, 1978
Brontë, Charlotte
Shirley, 1848/9
Browne, Mary
The Diary of a Girl in France in 1821, 1905

Caius, Johannes
Of English Dogges, the Diversities, the Names, the Natures and the Properties, 1576, 2nd. ed. 1880
Cooper, Thomas
The Life of Thomas Cooper, 1872
Cox, Alwyn and Angela
The Rockingham Works, Sheffield, 1974
Rockingham Pottery and Porcelain 1745–1842, 1983

Daniel, Rev. W. B.
Rural Sports, 1801–02
Darton, F. J. Harvey (ed.)
*The Life and Times of Mrs. Sherwood, c.*1911
Dudson, Audrey
Dudson: A family of potters since 1800, 1985
A Pottery Panorama: Dudson Bicentenary 1800–2000, 1999

Evelyn, John
Diary, covering most of his life (1620–1706), first published 1818

Flower, S.S
List of the Vertebrated Animals exhibited in the Gardens of the Zoological Society of London 1827–1927, Vol. 1. Mammals, 1929
Frith, A daughter of [W. Frith, the Victorian painter]
Leaves from a Life, published anonymously 1907

Godden, G.A.
An Illustrated Encyclopaedia of British Pottery and Porcelain, 1966
Minton Pottery and Porcelain of the First Period 1793–1850, 1968
Chamberlain Worcester Porcelain 1788–1852, 1982
(ed.), *Staffordshire Porcelain*, 1983
Grant of Rothiemurchus, Elizabeth (Mrs. Smith of Baltiboys)
(ed. Lady Strachey), *Memoirs of a Highland Lady*, 1911

Hare, A.J.C. (ed.)
Life and Letters of Maria Edgeworth, 1894
Harrison, William
Description of England, 1586
Haslem, John
The Old Derby China Factory, 1876
Hughes, G.B.
Collecting Antiques, 1949
Hutchinson's
Dog Encyclopaedia, *c.*1938

Ireland, Samuel
Graphic Illustrations of Hogarth, 1799

Jewitt, Llewellyn
Ceramic Art in Great Britain, 2 vols., 1878
Jones, Joan
Minton: The First Two Hundred Years of Design and Production, Shrewsbury, 1993

Lockett, T.A.
Davenport Pottery and Porcelain 1794–1887, Newton Abbot, 1972

MacDonogh, Katharine
Reigning Cats and Dogs, 1999

Oliver, Anthony
The Victorian Staffordshire Figure, 1971
Staffordshire Pottery, 1981

Pepys Samuel
Diary, 1660–1669
Pückler-Muskau, Prince
Tour in Germany, Holland and England in the Years 1826, 1827 and 1828 in a Series of Letters by a German Prince, 1833

Rice, Dennis G.
Rockingham Ornamental Porcelain, 1965
The Illustrated Guide to Rockingham Pottery and Porcelain, 1971
Derby Porcelain, The Golden Years 1750–70, 1983
English Porcelain Animals of the 19th Century, Woodbridge, 1989
Ritchie, Carson I.A.
The British Dog, 1981

Sandon, Henry
Royal Worcester Porcelain from 1862 to the Present Day, 1978
Sandon, Henry and John
Grainger's Worcester Porcelain, 1989
Secord, William
Dog Painting 1840–1940: The Social History of the Dog in Art, Woodbridge, 1992
Smith
On Rats, 1786
Stables, Gordon
Our Friend the Dog, 1895

Taplin, William
The Sportsman's Cabinet, 2 vols., 1803

Vivian, Margaret
Antique Collecting, 1937

Wedgwood, Josiah C.
Staffordshire Pottery and Its History, 1913
Wood, Rev. J.G.
The Illustrated Natural History, *c.*1850
Worde Wynkyn de
The Treatise perteyning to Hawkynge, Huntynge, &c emprynted at Wesmestre, 1496

Youatt, William
The Dog, 1854 edn.

Zoological Society
The Gardens and Menageries of the Zoological Society Delineated, 2 vols., 1831

Journals, Catalogues, Reports, Newspapers, Periodicals, etc.
Apollo, November 1987
Art Union, 1846
Catalogue of the Great Exhibition of 1851
Catalogue of the Exhibition of Staffordshire Porcelain 1740–1851, 1979
Collectors' Guide, March 1999
Connoisseur, The, 1908, 1915, 1916, 1918, 1922
Craftsman, The, 5 December 1730
Derby Porcelain International Society Journal 3
Grainger Lee & Co. Pattern Book
Minton Drawing Book
Potter's Examiner and Workman's Advocate, The, 11 May 1844
Report on the Employment of Children in Factories, 1843
Staffordshire Sentinel, November 1830
Theatre Royal, Worthing, Playbills, 18 and 22 October 1841

Index

The Antique Collectors' Club

The Antique Collectors' Club was formed in 1966 and quickly grew to a five figure membership spread throughout the world. It publishes the only independently run monthly antiques magazine, *Antique Collecting*, which caters for those collectors who are interested in widening their knowledge of antiques, both by greater awareness of quality and by discussion of the factors which influence the price that is likely to be asked. The Antique Collectors' Club pioneered the provision of information on prices for collectors and the magazine still leads in the provision of detailed articles on a variety of subjects.

It was in response to the enormous demand for information on 'what to pay' that the price guide series was introduced in 1968 with the first edition of *The Price Guide to Antique Furniture* (completely revised 1978 and 1989), a book which broke new ground by illustrating the more common types of antique furniture, the sort that collectors could buy in shops and at auctions rather than the rare museum pieces which had previously been used (and still to a large extent are used) to make up the limited amount of illustrations in books published by commercial publishers. Many other price guides have followed, all copiously illustrated, and greatly appreciated by collectors for the valuable information they contain, quite apart from prices. The Price Guide Series heralded the publication of many standard works of reference on art and antiques. *The Dictionary of British Art* (now in six volumes), *The Pictorial Dictionary of British 19th Century Furniture Design, Oak Furniture* and *Early English Clocks* were followed by many deeply researched reference works such as *The Directory of Gold and Silversmiths,* providing new information. Many of these books are now accepted as the standard work of reference on their subject.

The Antique Collectors' Club has widened its list to include books on gardens and architecture. All the Club's publications are available through bookshops world wide and a full catalogue of all these titles is available free of charge from the addresses below.

Club membership, open to all collectors, costs little. Members receive free of charge *Antique Collecting*, the Club's magazine (published ten times a year), which contains well-illustrated articles dealing with the practical aspects of collecting not normally dealt with by magazines. Prices, features of value, investment potential, fakes and forgeries are all given prominence in the magazine.

Among other facilities available to members are private buying and selling facilities and the opportunity to meet other collectors at their local antique collectors' clubs. There are over eighty in Britain and more than a dozen overseas. Members may also buy the Club's publications at special pre-publication prices.

As its motto implies, the Club is an organisation designed to help collectors get the most out of their hobby: it is informal and friendly and gives enormous enjoyment to all concerned.

For Collectors — By Collectors — About Collecting

ANTIQUE COLLECTORS' CLUB
Sandy Lane, Old Martlesham, Woodbridge, Suffolk IP12 4SD, UK
Tel: 01394 389950 Fax: 01394 389999
Email: sales@antique-acc.com Website: www.antique-acc.com
or
Market Street Industrial Park, Wappingers' Falls, NY 12590, USA
Tel: 845 297 0003 Fax: 845 297 0068
Email: info@antiquecc.com Website: www.antiquecc.com